SPANISH *for* GRINGOS

LEVEL 1　　　　　　**Fourth Edition**

WITHDRAWN

Shortcuts, Tips, and Secrets to Successful Learning

William C. Harvey, M.S.

BARRON'S

For all the gringos who try …

grin-go \ ˈgrin-(ˌ) gó\ *n, pl* **gringos** [Sp, alter. of *griego* Greek, stranger, fr. L *Graecus* Greek] (1849): a foreigner in Spain or Latin America esp. when of English or American origin …

By permission. From *Merriam-Webster's Collegiate® Dictionary, 11th Edition* © 2015 by Merriam-Webster, Inc. (www.Merriam-Webster.com).

About the Author

William C. Harvey is founder of Language Services Institute, a highly-successful conversational Spanish program aimed specifically at meeting the needs of today's busy adult learner. For the past 20 years he has taught Spanish and ESL (English as a Second Language) in school districts and community colleges, as well as in private industry. He has also traveled extensively throughout the West Coast giving workshops and seminars to teachers and professional organizations. Mr. Harvey holds a bachelor's degree in Spanish and a master's degree in Bilingual-Bicultural Education from Cal State University, Fullerton, where he received the "Project of the Year" award for his work in ESL Curriculum Development. Bill has written several books for Barron's, including *Spanish for Law Enforcement, Household Spanish, Spanish for Healthcare Professionals,* and *Spanish for Educators.*

All inquiries should be addressed to:
Barron's Educational Series, Inc.
250 Wireless Boulevard
Hauppauge, NY 11788
www.barronseduc.com

ISBN: 978-1-4380-7529-7

Library of Congress Catalog Card No. 2015944803

Printed in the United States of America
9 8 7 6 5 4 3 2 1

CONTENTS

Hola, fellow gringos!

Finally, after years of teaching classroom Spanish using the dreadful "textbook approach," I got fed up and decided to try something different. Having picked up Spanish myself by hanging around non-English speakers, I'd discovered what gringos *really* needed to learn *el español*. So I put together a series of practical, easy-to-follow shortcuts, tips, and secrets to success—designed specifically for folks who aren't interested in "studying" a foreign language. In place of traditional units and lessons, *Spanish for Gringos* is intended as a guidebook and offers nothing more than helpful suggestions. This approach should make your language learning experience easy and *muy divertido* (lots of fun)!

Adiós for now,

Bill

Reasons Why Spanish Is Easy to Learn

Other languages are great, but believe me—I've chosen Spanish because it is the easiest of them all. I've spent my life developing *Spanish for Gringos* for six very good reasons.

1 Spanish is a lot like English.

Most Spanish words have the same Latin-based form as their English equivalents. Many words in both languages look and sound almost the same, which makes guessing a breeze.

2 Spanish is not complicated.

Conversations in Spanish can be kept short and sweet. Complex messages are often exchanged using only a few simple words. Only an understanding of basic grammar and pronunciation patterns is needed for successful communication to take place.

3 It's OK if you blow it.

Spanish speakers enjoy helping gringos who try. Hispanics are generally proud, warm-hearted people who admire those with a sincere interest in learning their native tongue. So cheer up. Lousy Spanish only makes *you* feel stupid.

4 Spanish is not hard to practice.

All across the nation, the Hispanic population continues to grow at a tremendous rate. Regular exposure to Spanish should not be a major problem. Neither should it be difficult for the learner to find someone to "practice with." Also remember that lots of Spanish still lies just south of the border.

5 Spanish can be profitable.

American business people have discovered that buying and selling in more than one language makes good business sense. And with Hispanics in the United States now spending millions a day, their market has become a primary target of corporate America. Increasingly, companies are providing Spanish training for employees. And better pay seems to make learning that much easier. So revise that résumé! Learning Spanish can lead to financial success.

6 Spanish is fun to learn.

There's nothing like the thrill of speaking Spanish and being understood for the first time. Or the *second* time. It's not long before gringos get "hooked." Maybe it's because communication in a new language allows you to meet, understand, and assist more people. That does wonders for the self-image. Spanish also can make life more fun. In traveling to Spanish-speaking countries, common activities such as shopping and dining suddenly become more enjoyable and exciting. A second language is like a new toy—so play with it! After mastering Spanish you will find that similar languages, like French and Italian, are easier to learn. And don't worry about staying motivated. It seems that once gringos get rolling in *español*, they're usually very difficult to stop!

"Who Needs It?"

Spanish for Gringos is not *for everyone.*

For those of you who plan on living in Spain or Latin America and need extensive language training ... I'm sorry. And to those who already speak Spanish and are looking to improve their reading and writing skills ... I apologize. You see, this guidebook was *not* written for people whose intentions are to "study."

Spanish for Gringos is for everybody else.

Most of what you'll find here is basic, practical information that you can use right away, with a lot of the technical "stuff" trimmed away. Generalizations about Spanish are made. Translations are not "precise." And the primary theme is to *assist gringos only*, as they begin communication with Spanish speakers at work or at play.

Although this guidebook should help any Spanish learners, it is basically *an orientation to the type of Spanish that is commonly spoken here in the United States.*

Before You Begin

OK, *brace yourselves!* This guidebook contains *no* drills, *no* worksheets, and *no* tests!

… Instead, learners will be asked to follow some
RATHER UNUSUAL GUIDELINES

- **Forget what you've been told!** (You'll just get hung-up on useless details.) There's no such thing as perfect Spanish, so don't get stuck trying to figure out the best way to say something. This book gives you only what you *need* to know. Instead of traditional grammar and pronunciation practice, try the practical shortcuts, tips, and secrets to success. If you follow the useful suggestions, you'll be all right most of the time.

- **Spend most of your time listening!** (You'll be talking in no time.) To learn the way a baby learns language, it's important to "take in" lots of Spanish at the beginning. Listen to fluent speakers. Soon, new words will emerge naturally in everyday conversation. Use the one-liners and greetings freely, but don't force speech until you feel ready to speak. Online language programs, DVDs, mobile apps, and interactive CDs can be helpful. But real-life practice is better!

- **Act as if you know more than you do!** (You'll soon believe that you *are* fluent.) Learn to have self-confidence around people who speak only Spanish. Even if you don't understand a word, smile and laugh a lot. "Concentrate" when you are asked a question, and always answer with a short response. Imitate verbal and nonverbal expressions. Be assertive, yet remain friendly. Experiment with new words and phrases. Fake it, and you'll be speaking Spanish *pronto!*

- **Don't make excuses!** (You'll never get started if you do.) Thanks to modern research, we now know that the following statements about language learning are Untrue!

You need to do grammar exercises . . . . *No!*
You need to develop good pronunciation . . . . *No!*
You need to start at an early age . . . . *No!*
You need to memorize vocabulary lists . . . . *No!*
You need to be "good at languages" . . . . *No!*

So there! The truth is you have *no excuse* and ...
You *will* learn Spanish quickly and easily . . . . *Sí!*

- **Most of all, relax!** The idea of learning a new language scares the life out of most people, so don't feel ashamed. Just accept the fact that you're going to sound strange and look awkward for a while. It's no big deal. This guidebook is designed to relieve you of stress and frustration. Never give up! Don't worry about a thing, have some fun, and just go for it. With *Spanish for Gringos*, learning *no es problema*.

Checklist

1   **Comfortable chair**   ☐
2   **Background music**   ☐
3   **Favorite beverage**   ☐
4   **Laid-back attitude**   ☐

1

CHAPTER *UNO*

¿Habla español?

(Do You Speak Spanish?)

Spanish Words Most Gringos Already Know:

americano

amigo

amor

español

se habla inglés

loco

macho

padre

rodeo

pueblo

rancho

señor

señorita

fiesta

cha-cha-cha

el tango

olé

quesadilla

burrito

chile

enchilada

salsa

taco

latino

gringo

chiquita

zorro

cerveza

margarita

tequila

vino

bueno

grande

mucho

más

adiós

gracias

Feliz Navidad

hasta la vista

por favor

pronto

sí

dinero

uno

dos

tres

piñata

cucaracha

no problema

Los Angeles

hombre

bravo

Spanglish

A unique blend of Spanish and English has gradually evolved in the United States as more and more Spanish speakers and English speakers have made attempts to communicate. Nationwide, Spanglish is alive and well (though words may vary from region to region). You see, many English words either can't be exactly translated into Spanish or are just easier to say when mixed with English. What's great is that they all sound like words gringos know. Check out these easy-to-remember "Spanish Englishisms":

> **NOTE**
> Spanglish is not street slang! But it's *not Spanish*, either. So some people may make comments. Be prepared!

SPANGLISH	ENGLISH	SPANISH
bloquear	to block	*obstruir*
cachar	to catch	*coger*
chequear	to check	*revisar*
craquear	to crack	*romper*
cuitiar	to quit	*renunciar*
lonchar	to lunch	*almorzar*
parquear	to park	*estacionar*
taipiar	to type	*escribir a máquina*
wachar	to watch	*mirar*
textear	to text	*mandar texto*

Did you know? Mixing both languages when "you can't remember" is still OK!

HOT TIP!

If it's close—they'll probably get it! Since Spanglish and English are so similar, you really don't need to worry about pronunciation.

SPANGLISH	ENGLISH	SPANISH
la baika	bike	*la bicicleta*
las brekas	brakes	*los frenos*
la carpeta	carpet	*la alfombra*
el lonche	lunch	*el almuerzo*
la marqueta	market	*el mercado*
el mofle	muffler	*el silenciador*
el pay	pie	*el pastel*
el raite	ride	*un paseo*
la troca	truck	*el camión*
la yarda	yard	*el patio*

NOTE
Don't struggle with the pronunciation of Spanish words yet! You'll be getting the "Secrets to Soundmaking" shortly.

la iPad	los Levis
el Hilton	el Kleenex
los Pampers	la Budweiser

HOT TIP!

Are you aware that names of people, cities, streets, buildings, companies, and brand names are *not* usually translated into Spanish?

Vamos a Chicago.   Let's go to Chicago.
El señor Rubio habla español.   Mister Rubio speaks Spanish.
Trabajo en el Marriott.   I work at the Marriott.

Understanding Spanish Speakers

You're right. It does sound like one long word. Everything is too fast. So what's a gringo to do? Well, don't panic. Relax, take a deep breath, smile, and try these **Five Secrets to Success:**

1 Focus on the message.

Listen for key words and how they're expressed, instead of trying to understand *the whole enchilada*. Are they asking or telling you something? Focus on the tone of their voice. Avoid translating each word. Concentrate on the main idea only.

2 Use your hands and face.

Express comprehension by pointing, moving, or touching things. Make faces. Write or draw what you think they're trying to say. Be as expressive as you can. Soon, they'll get into the act. Don't give up, and you'll eventually end up communicating with *no problemas*.

3 Say: *Más despacio, por favor.*

(Mahs dehs-pah'-see-oh, pohr fah-bohr') which means: "More slowly please." Or say *¿Qué?* (keh) and *¿Cómo?* (koh'-moh) which means "What?" and "How's that?"

4 Listen for the English.

Since both languages are Latin based, many Spanish words sound a lot like English. Guess and you'll probably be right!

5 Relax and try again.

Swallow your pride and remember—they're having as much trouble as you are. Lighten up, keep it fun, believe in yourself, and *español* will begin to make sense.

Hey, Listen!
(¡Escuche!)

Don't say a word! You don't have to. Much like children learn their native tongue, it's best to *listen first!* So don't force yourself to speak. After listening to Spanish for a while, *it will gradually start coming out of you!* For now, try some of these easy (and inexpensive) ways to pick up on those new "foreign noises":

- Listen to Spanish radio stations (check local listings).
- Find out which TV stations also air in Spanish.
- Watch Spanish movies (with English subtitles).
- Search for Spanish downloads, podcasts, and video clips.
- Ride city buses or subways through Spanish-speaking areas.
- See a Spanish language play or musical performance.
- Attend a Spanish-speaking religious service of your faith.
- Join a Spanish-speaking club, team, or organization.
- Check into travel packages to Spain or Latin America.
- Befriend those Spanish speakers whom you see regularly.
- Take a Spanish class, or buy a program with lots of online practice.
- Download a Spanish learning app.
- Shop or dine at places where Spanish is spoken all around you.
- Keep going, and try to be creative:

_____

_____

_____

_____

_____

HOT TIP!

You can obviously add your own ideas to this list. But however you choose to *escuchar* (listen), always remember the three **C**s: **C**alm down, Observe **C**losely, and **C**oncentrate on what's being said!

The "Nonverbals"

Guess what? If you'd like to communicate in Spanish, but don't feel like speaking, there's an easy and fun way to send messages. As with most cultures, certain *hand signals, facial expressions, eye contact,* and *body language* convey valuable meaning. Here are some of my favorite hand signals from Mexico.

I love it! Talk without speaking!

Venga.
Come here.

By moving your hand (or arm) in a downward motion, you're calling someone to you.

Un momento.
Just a moment.

By putting your thumb and index finger together, you're telling someone, "Hold on just a moment. I'll be right with you."

No gracias.
No thanks.

By moving your pointer finger back and forth, you're telling someone "No" or "Don't."

More nonverbals

Touching your elbow while looking at folks is the same as calling them tightwads or "cheap."

NOTE
If you know how to say the words, add them for emphasis.

¡*Ojo!*
Beware!

Pointing to your eye means "Be careful" or "Watch out!"

¡*Qué grande!*
How big!

Always point upwards, with palm side of the hand toward you, when referring to the height of a person ...

... and outwards, palm-side-down, when referring to the height of an object or animals.

NOTE
There are many more, so take time to observe people as they interact. Ask the meanings if you're not sure. Practice the nonverbals and you'll be able to "communicate" right away!

¿*Puede recordarlo?*
Can You Remember It?

I know we have just begun, but why not stop and review a moment before moving on to the next chapter. Just answer as many questions as you can!

- Give at least two reasons why Spanish is easy to learn.
- What are some of the guidelines to learn Spanish quickly?
- Name five Spanish words you knew before reading this book.
- What is *Spanglish?*
- How can you get folks to slow down when they are speaking Spanish very fast?
- List two activities that can help you practice listening to Spanish.
- Give a "hand signal" in Spanish.

2

CHAPTER *DOS*

Las primeras palabras

(The First Words)

Secrets to Soundmaking

Basically, you need to know only *five* primary Spanish sounds (the vowels) that will make you comprehensible and help you to understand more. When speaking Spanish, if you make the following sounds every time the corresponding letter appears, you'll sound just like a native speaker. When? *Every time the letter appears!* Try making these sounds toward the front of your mouth instead of the back—with little or no air coming out. Short, choppy sounds are better than long, stretched-out ones. Go ahead, practice now that nobody's listening and soon you will be able to impress your friends!

Trust me! Know these and you will be on your way!

a (ah)	like y**a**cht
e (eh)	like m**e**t
i (ee)	like k**ee**p
o (oh)	like **o**pen
u (oo)	like sp**oo**n

HOT TIP!

Exactness doesn't matter! As I said before—if it's close, they'll probably get it. Besides, the goal of this guidebook is getting people to communicate, *not* teaching all the different Spanish sounds. So stop fretting. You sound great to me!

The Big Five

a   *banana, cucaracha, cha-cha-cha, mañana*
e   *tres, excelente, olé, elefante, nene*
i   *sí, dividir, Trini, Miami, Lidia*
o   *loco, ocho, no, Colorado, dos*
u   *Lulú, mucho, tú, burro, Uruguay*

The "Others"

Easy enough. But what about the *other* sounds in Spanish—such as the consonants? Good news—they're not much different from English. But here are a few that may cause confusion.

c has two sounds: c^1 like **c**at and c^2 like **c**elery, when followed by **e** or **i**.
g also has two sounds: g^1 (g) like **g**o and g^2 (h) like **h**ello, when followed by **e** or **i**.
h   (*Don't* pronounce it; like **k** in knife.)
j (h)   like **h**ot
ll (y)   like **y**es
ñ (ny)   like can**y**on
qu (k)   like **k**iss
v (b)   like **b**reak
z (s)   like **s**it

HOT TIPS!

- These 8 are the only "toughies." The rest can be pronounced the *same as English!*
- Take note! Gringos have the most trouble with **qu**.

> More volume! I can't hear you.

- Like the Big Five, these sounds have *no exceptions!* In Spanish, respective sounds are always the same *every time their corresponding letter appears!*
- Don't worry about your "regional accent." Making yourself understood in Spanish doesn't depend on what part of the United States *you* are from.

Now, let's try to put all these "pieces of noise" together. Refer back to the Secrets to Soundmaking as you read the following (**ALOUD**):

c^1	*coco, carro, Colorado, capitán*
c^2	*Cecilia, cigarro, centro, cilantro*
g^1	*gorila, garaje, guacamole, Paraguay*
g^2	*general, Geraldo, gimnasio, rígido*
h	*huevo, hombre, hola, ahora*
j	*Juan, trabajo, frijoles, Julio*
ll	*llama, millón, tortillas, amarillo*
ñ	*señor, mañana, español, piña colada*
qu	*poquito, qué pasa, tequila, quesadilla*
v	*vino, Victoria, viva, hasta la vista*
z	*López, cerveza, Venezuela, González*

Here's a great way to practice some of your new Spanish sounds. Simply read each word aloud, and look up their meanings in English later on:

HOT TIPS!

- Always try to "visualize" Spanish words because they're spelled exactly as you say them. And **don't worry about what you sound like!**
- **Run 'em- together …** What's really nice about the *español* is that it's put together in little pieces—just like the *inglés*. So, to sound like a native speaker, **thefasterthebetter!**
- **Read 'em Right!** By now, you've probably noticed the little accent mark ( ) on parts of certain words. Don't get nervous. It only means that you're supposed to say that part of the word **LOUDER!**

*Ma-**rí**-a*

Forget about the accent mark on little words, like *sí* or *qué!* That's just how they're spelled!

SOUNDS	PRONOUNCED	PRACTICE WORDS		
que	keh	*pequeño*	*porque*	*queso*
qui	kee	*chiquito*	*quiero*	*quién*
		máquina	*parquímetro*	*mosquito*
ji or *gi*	hee	*jinete*	*gigante*	*jirafa*
		girasol	*tejido*	*rugido*
je or *ge*	heh	*gemelos*	*jefe*	*gente*
		objeto	*tijeras*	*jeringa*
gue	geh	*guerra*	*manguera*	*juguete*
gui	ghee	*guitarra*	*guisantes*	*seguir*
		águila	*alguien*	*amiguito*
ce	seh	*cebolla*	*ceja*	*cárcel*
ci	see	*cine*	*capacidad*	*cocido*
lle	yeh	*lleno*	*ballena*	*calle*
lli	yee	*trillizos*	*allí*	*pollito*
lla	yah	*silla*	*olla*	*llamar*
llo	yoh	*bello*	*llorar*	*sillón*
llu	yoo	*lluvia*	*velludo*	

¡ANUNCIO IMPORTANTE!

Once you become familiar with the different Spanish sounds you'll make the *first giant step toward fluency!* So why not go back and read the section on "Soundmaking" again!

Más Pronunciation Details!

- If there's *no* accent mark, say the *last part* of the word louder (espa**ñ**ol).
- For words ending in a vowel, *n* or *s*, the *second to the last* part of the word is emphasized (enchi**la**da).
- With **rr**, roll your Rs—but *only* if you can. They'll understand if you use **r** instead.
- The **d** sometimes sounds like our "th" (as in "this") in the middle and at the end of words. Try it: nada, todo, adiós, libertad.
- People from Spanish-speaking countries don't all sound alike, but they all understand one another and will usually understand you.
- Forget "rules." They'll only make it worse!
- Check out the 10 Most Common Gringo Pronunciation Errors on page 154.

NOTE
You won't find any more pronunciation "guides" next to words in this book. Instead, learn the "Secrets to Soundmaking" and practice in "real-life" situations!

Spanish Words That Don't Need Translating

There are literally thousands of Spanish words that are easy to understand. All you have to do is focus on **the English within.**
No need to translate these:

Go ahead—
read each one aloud!

EASY

aplicación	favorito	operación
arte	fotografía	persona
béisbol	importancia	policía
café	inteligente	posesión
cámara	interesante	posible
comercial	limón	refrigerador
conversación	mapa	teléfono
escuela	millonario	televisión
especial	minuto	turismo
estúpido	momento	universidad
familia	nervioso	vacación
fantástico	noviembre	vocabulario

The EASIEST

banana	hockey	natural
chocolate	horrible	plaza
color	hospital	popular
doctor	hotel	radio
final	idea	taxi
golf	individual	terror

Other Easy to Remember Words

diccionario	instrumento	programa
dieta	moderno	presidente
dólar	música	reservación
eléctrico	producto	sincero
elegante	profesional	violento
información	sexo	restaurante

Mi buena memoria (My good memory)

Start today! Make a *lista* of Spanish words (without looking back) that you already have "picked up." You'll be surprised.

_____

_____

_____

_____

_____

_____

_____

HOT TIPS!

- **Remember:** *No pain-no gain!* As in all stretching exercises, when you pronounce this stuff, *make it hurt! Use those "mouth muscles"!*
- **Spanish sounds a bit like English**—but with an accent!
- **Be careful!** Some Spanish words look like English—but aren't. For example, *contestar* (to answer) has nothing to do with contests. And *pan* (bread) or *pie* (foot) could cause confusion!

¡ATENCIÓN!

"Add" an upside-down mark in front of *Exclamations* and *Questions*

Do you understand?   *¿Comprende?*
Yes! I understand!   *¡Sí! ¡Yo comprendo!*

Speak Up! (¡Hable!)

> ¡Hola Ramón!
> ¿Qué pasa?

> Yo...er...
> mumble...
> mumble..
> mumble...

> **Again:** *Don't worry* about "sounding dumb." All that matters is that you somehow manage to *understand* each other!

Muchos Ways to Practicar

Listening to Spanish was no big deal. The next step, then, is to practice *saying* something. Once you've warmed up with Spanish words that resemble English, try these practice techniques for improving pronunciation, while picking up the hard-to-remember stuff:

- Next time you're at an Hispanic restaurant, order food for everyone at the table.
- Travel through Spanish-speaking sections of town and say aloud the words on billboards and store windows. (You may get funny looks!)
- Randomly open books on the Southwest, Latin America, or Spain, and try pronouncing all the Spanish words you find.
- Next time you're alone, try reading English aloud—but use the Spanish Secrets to Soundmaking! Don't laugh—it works!
- Start slowly. Try practicing *one sound a week!*
- Record yourself regularly while reading Spanish language articles, stories, or other reading material.
- If possible, buy some language DVDs, CDs, or apps and work with them.
- Get on the Internet and search for a Spanish-speaking chatroom or blog. Find out all the ways to interact online with your Spanish-speaking friends.
- Again, there is nothing better than speaking face to face with a Spanish-speaker. Are you willing to try?

HOT TIP!

The best way to learn a new language is to talk face to face with someone. Think of convenient ways to learn Spanish from Hispanic people. One popular method is to offer a little English instruction in return.

Baby's First *Palabras* (Words)

We've already taken a look at *Words Gringos Already Know* and *Should Know*. Now it's time to try words and phrases you *have to know*. In the same way a baby learns "survival words" at first, it's best to start with the Spanish that will take you the farthest. The following seem to be the words acquired first in any language. Use them to communicate complete messages. (**Wait!** Check back on the Secrets to Soundmaking!)

HOT TIPS!

Before we go on, here are a few helpful suggestions on how to use these first *palabras*.

- Do speak in "broken" Spanish, by putting only key words together. Just "mumble" the less important stuff. (We'll learn more about this later!)
- If you can't remember a word, try another way to explain yourself.
- Try out *one word a day* and build from there. Gain confidence by starting off with those you like best.
- Develop a system for remembering. Play "word-picture" association games.
- Let others correct you. It's OK! Natural mistakes help you learn faster.
- For words you use a lot, it might be a good idea to learn others that mean the same thing.
- Don't forget that dialects may vary. You're going to encounter *muchas más palabras* that won't be mentioned here!

Hola.

agua	water
amigo	friend
baño	bathroom
bueno	good
carro	car
casa	house
comida	food
dinero	money
grande	big
hombre	man
más	more
mucho	a lot
mujer	woman
muy bien	very well
niño	child
nombre	name
número	number
persona	person
teléfono	phone
trabajo	work
por favor	please
gracias	thanks
hola	Hi!
adiós	Bye!
ropa	clothing

Put two or more together!
y = and
o = or
pero = but
¡Gracias y adiós!

These words are grasped early also: *Señor (Sr.)* is a "Mr."; *Señora (Sra.)* is a "Mrs."; *Señorita (Srta.)* is a "Miss." *Sorry,* there is no word for "Ms."—**yet!**

So, how's your soundmaking?

My Favorite First Words

Here are more gems that work all by themselves.

algo something	*alguien* someone
ahora mismo or *ahorita* right now	*los demás* the rest of them
después afterwards	*ninguno* none of them
antes before	*cualquiera* any of them
mientras during	*cada uno* each one
entonces then	*ambos* both of them
ya already	*algunos* some
demasiado too much	*varios* several
otra another	*nada* nothing
otra vez again	*siguiente* the next one
casi almost	*mismo* the same
juntos together	*diferente* different
solo alone	*primero* first
todo all of it	*último* last
nadie no one	*en todas partes* everywhere

HOT TIPS!

- To really impress, just greet with: *¡Buenos!* (daytime) or *¡Buenas!* (late afternoon and evening).
- Instead of *Adiós* (Good-bye), try *Nos vemos* (We'll see ya), or

Hasta (Until) {
luego (later)
mañana (tomorrow)
la vista (next time)
}

- Find some more and have fun!

The Greetings and Stuff

Having any problems in getting started? Your troubles are over. Memorize these as one long word and they'll think you're fluent!

¡Hola! ¡Qué tal!   Hi! How's it going?

Buenos días.   Good morning

Buenas tardes.   Good afternoon

Buenas noches.   Good evening or Good night

¡Adiós!   Bye!

More Courtesies

"Hello?"

¿Aló?, *¿Bueno?* or *¿Diga?* are all good when you answer the phone. "Who's calling?" is *¿De parte de quién?*

"Who's There?"

When you knock and want to enter, it's *¿Se puede?* (Can I come in?). To say "Come in!" use: *¡Pase!* or *¡Adelante!*

"Thanks!"

Instead of the old, *Muchas gracias* for "Thanks a lot," try these stronger words of appreciation: **¡Muchísimas gracias! ¡Mil gracias!** or the one I use: **¡Muy amable!**

Por favor is "please."
De nada is "you're welcome."
Lo siento is "I'm sorry."

> Remember that Spanish speakers exchange greetings regularly. Try learning other ways folks say hello, and don't be afraid to "greet" someone back!

"Excuse Me!"

Whenever you'd like to get through a crowd, use *¡Con permiso!* If you cough or sneeze, say: *¡Perdón!* To get someone's attention, try: *¡Disculpe! ¡Pase!* is "Go ahead!" *¡Salud!* is "Bless you!" Keep in mind that having good manners is very important in building new relationships!

 vs.

¿Qué pasa?

This is the standard "What's happening?" Sometimes you'll be greeted with *¿Qué ...* (and something else)? Don't worry! They're still only asking what's going on. Here's the easy way out: always answer with—"*¡Sin novedad!*" or "*¡Nada!*" (Nothing new!)

¿Cómo está usted?

Everyone knows this one. It means, "How are you?" And as with *¿Qué pasa?*, when you hear, *¿Cómo ...* (something)? you can "sneak by" using the classic, *¡Muy bien!* (Just fine!)

> **NOTE**
> Later on, we'll take a look at other ways to answer these *¿Qué ...?* and *¿Cómo ...?* questions.

Las presentaciones
(Introductions)

There are many ways to say, "Nice to meet you!" but the most common is *¡Mucho gusto!* During the introduction, don't forget to shake the other person's hand. If something is said to *you* first, smile and say, *¡igualmente!*, which translates to, "Same to you."

¿Cómo se llama? (What's your name?) and *Me llamo* _____. (My name is _____). are also nice to know!

Even if you make a mistake, smiling always leaves a good impression!

HOT TIPS!

- *¿Y usted?* means, "And you?"
- *¿Qué pasó?* is "What's the matter?" or "What happened?"
- And mind your manners!

¿Dónde está?
(Where is it?)

More than likely, the very first question you'll get asked will be, "Where's the bathroom?" (Whenever anyone needs directions, they'll use, *¿Dónde está...?*) Here, then, is what you'll need:

... *a la derecha* = to the right
... *a la izquierda* = to the left
... *adelante* or *derecho* or *recto* = straight ahead
... *aquí* or *acá* = here
... *ahí* = there
... *allá* = over there

NOTE
Watch and listen for *está!* See if you can guess how it's used.

¡*Viva el vocabulario!* (Long Live Vocabulary!)

Following are three groups of words most folks seem to pick up and use almost immediately.

Los números
(The numbers)

0	*cero*
1	*uno*
2	*dos*
3	*tres*
4	*cuatro*
5	*cinco*
6	*seis*
7	*siete*
8	*ocho*
9	*nueve*

Los colores
(The colors)

black	*negro*
blue	*azul*
brown	*café*
gray	*gris*
green	*verde*
orange	*anaranjado*
purple	*morado*
red	*rojo*
white	*blanco*
yellow	*amarillo*

La clase
(The class)

el libro		*la mesa*	
el lápiz		*la computadora*	
la pluma		*la tableta*	
el papel		*el escritorio*	
el cuaderno		*la silla*	
la pizarra		*el cesto de basura*	

CHOOSE 'n USE   Here are some sentences that will help you put these words to practice. Fill in the blanks, read each sentence aloud, and plan ways to use them in real-life situations.

- **Los números**

  Mi número de teléfono es...   My telephone number is ... (542-8763, etc.).

  ¿Dónde está el cuarto número ...?   Where's room number ... (five, three, etc.)?

- **Los colores**

  Me gusta el color ...   I like the color ... (purple, red, etc.).
  ¿Es ... o ...?   Is it ... (black, etc.) or ... (white, etc.)?
  Hay algunos de color ...   There are some ... (orange, etc.) ones.

- **La clase**

  ¿Tiene usted un/una ...   Do you have a ... (pen, book, etc.)?

  ... está en ...   The ... (paper, notebook, etc.) is "in," "on," or "at" the ... (desk, table, etc.).

  Necesito ...   I need the ... (computer, chair, etc.).

At the end of this book you'll discover a Personal Success Chart. Use it! Simply pencil in your "experiences." Try out your new skills regularly. See how fast your **lista** can grow!

¿Puede recordarlo?
(Can You Remember It?)

- Pronounce the five vowels in Spanish (The Big Five!).
- Write three Spanish words that are spelled the same in English.
- Name one way you plan to practice "speaking" Spanish.
- Give one expression in Spanish that is used to greet someone.
- Say the numbers 1 through 9 in Spanish.

3

CHAPTER *TRES*

Más, Más, Más
(More, More, More)

This is how you say "The."

The *El* and *La* Business

If you want to name a single object or person, put either *el* (masculine) or *la* (feminine) in front. It may seem strange, but as you continue to learn more *español*, you will need to know the meanings of "masculine" and "feminine." In Spanish, single objects require either an *el* or a *la* in front. This has nothing to do with an object's sex! It's just the *el* and *la* Business! In order to remember which one to use, just check to see if the word ends in either an *o* (generally masculine) or an *a* (generally feminine). People are easy because males get "*el*" and females get "*la*":

el

el ta**co**
el ami**go**
el bur**ro**

HOT TIPS!

- A few words are weird (i.e., *el sofá, la mano, el problema*).
- Some words don't end in **o** or **a** (i.e., *el elefante, la paz*), so you'll have to memorize them.
- *El* and *la* refer not only to male and female persons (i.e., *el señor, la dama*), but to animals as well.
- *It doesn't matter* if you get confused and use the wrong one, *you'll still be understood!* So don't hold back!

la

la enchilad**a**
la señorit**a**
la cucarach**a**

More *El/La* Business and *Un/Una*

The following are common questions and answers about one part of Spanish that is completely foreign to English.

1 Can *el* and *la* also refer to more than one person, animal or thing?

No way, José. Two or more *tacos* and *enchiladas* become:
los *tacos* and **las** *enchiladas*

> Notice what happens to *el*. More than *uno* is *los*.
>
> See? You've got to tag on the "s" at the end.

2 How do I say "a" or "an" instead of "the"?

At times in English we use "a" or "an" to say "any old thing." In Spanish, use **un** or **una**:
un *taco* and **una** *enchilada* are "a" taco and "an" enchilada.

> And guess what? **Unos** and **unas** mean "some."

3 Why is this aspect of Spanish a little confusing?

The answer is simple: You're not used to it yet! Grasping these concepts may take a little time. Besides, your messing up Spanish won't make much difference! Your listeners will figure out what you said anyway. But if you do "get corrected" just say to yourself—"I'll get it right the next time!"

HOT TIPS!

- Words (naming things, people, or concepts) that have the following endings, *usually* need *la* (feminine) in front.
  = *a*
  = *sión*
  = *tad*
  = *ción*
  = *dad*
  = *umbre*
  = *ambre*
- By the way, *él*, with an accent mark means "he."
- *uno* is "one" also!
- Talking about "more than one" (plurals) is a lot like *inglés*:
  cuatro tacos
  four tacos
  cinco relojes
  five watches

The Once-and-for-All Rule

HOT TIPS!

- You can expect to get the hang of this *rápido!*
- Matching the **o**'s and *a*'s works great with *"Los colores"!*: *Muchos carros blancos* Many white cars; **But:** *muchos carros azules*

As we've learned, talking about "more than one" (plural) in Spanish is very much as it is in English; (*un taco → dos tacos*). Words not ending in a vowel take **es** at the end; *un doctor → dos doctóres*).

What isn't like English is what I call the "Once-and-for-all Rule." You see, not only do all Spanish words that name (nouns) or describe (adjectives) things, people, or concepts need "s," or "es" to make them plural but when they are used together, the **o**'s and **a**'s (masculine and feminine) must match:

*Much**os** tac**os** delicios**os***   Many delicious tacos
y and
*Much**as** enchilad**as** delicios**as***   Many delicious enchiladas

---

NOTA IMPORTANTE

Muchos means "many."
Mucho means "a great deal" or "a lot." ... And don't confuse *mucho* with *muy,* which means "very."

poco   a little bit   *poquito*   a very little bit
pocos   a few   *poquitos*   very few

Did you notice?
= *ito* and = *ita* word endings reduce things.

The "One-a-Day" One-liners

A very good way to gain confidence while learning a new language is to speak in short, meaningful phrases. Instead of struggling with the formation of correct long sentences, expressive one-liners can be used—especially when there's really nothing left to say. And using them will make you feel more confident! You'll sound more fluent than you actually are. Practice a new one every day … (Careful! They're addictive!)

Use these phrases whenever you think it might be appropriate.

¡Por supuesto!   Of course!
¡Quizás!   Maybe!
¡Me alegro!   I'm so glad!
¡Es verdad!   That's the truth!
¡Más o menos!   More or less!
¿Está bien?   Is that OK?
¡Creo que sí!   I think so!
¡Cómo no!   Why not!
¡Es posible!   It's possible!
¡Claro!   Sure!
¡De acuerdo!   I agree!
¡Sin duda!   No doubt!
¡Depende!   That depends!
¡A lo contrario!   On the contrary!

¡Buena idea!   Good idea!
¡Yo también!   Me, too!
¡Yo tampoco!   Me, neither!
¡Ojalá!   I hope so!
¡Ya veo!   I see!
¿Quién sabe?   Who knows?
¿Está seguro(a)?   Are you [he/she] sure?
¿Así?   Like this?
¡Lo que (usted) quiera!   Whatever you want!
¡Tanto mejor!   All the better!
¡Con razón!   No wonder!
¡Está bueno!   That's good!

For Busy *Personas*

¡Ya me voy!   I'm leaving now!
¡Ya se fue!   He or she has left!
¡Ahora vengo!   I'll be right back!
¡Ahí viene!   Here he or she comes!
¿Listo?   Ready?

HOT TIPS!

- Caution! Rudeness will ruin communication!
- These one-liners are great at *fiestas*! Here, for example, is a bit of one-liner dialogue.
  Maria: *¿Listo?* (Ready?)
  Carlos: *Creo que sí. ¿Y Tomás?* (I think so. And Thomas?)
  Maria: *¡Ahí viene!* (Here he comes!)
  Carlos: *¿Y Carolina?* (And Carolina?)
  Maria: *¡Ya se fue!* (She's left!)
  Carlos: *¡Está bueno!* (That's good!)

Más One-liners

No entiendo or *No comprendo.*
    I don't understand.
A la vez.   At the same time.
Muchas veces.   Lots of times.
Una vez.   One time.

No sé.   I don't know.

Todavía no.   Not yet.
Ahora no.   Not now.
En punto.   On time.

Al revés.   Backwards.
Boca abajo.   Upside down.

These expressions are also used instead of *adiós.*

¡*Vaya con Dios!*   Go with God!
¡*Dios le bendiga!*   God bless you!
¡*Buen viaje!*   Have a nice trip!
Solude a ... de mi parte   Give my
    regards to …
¡*Tenga buen día!*   Have a nice day!
¡*Chau!*   Bye!

Use these expressions, but with *emoción* (emotion)!

¡*Felicitaciones!*   Congratulations!
¡*Feliz Navidad!*   Merry Christmas!
¡*Feliz cumpleaños!*   Happy Birthday!

¡*Socorro!*   Help!
¡*Caramba!*   Wow!
¡*Dios mío!*   For heaven's sake!

¡*Mentiras!*   Lies!
¡*Basta!*   Enough!
¡*Vaya!*   Go on!
¡*Vamos!*   Let's go!
¡*Buena suerte!*   Good luck!
¡*Salud!*   Cheers!
¡*Mi más sentido pésame!*   Accept my condolences!

Es muy ...
It's very ...

cierto	certain
correcto	correct
fantástico	fantastic
importante	important
interesante	interesting
necesario	necessary
obvio	obvious
terrible	terrible
difícil	difficult

¡Qué ...

barbaridad!	How awful!
bueno!	How great!
chiste!	What a joke!
disfrute!	Have a good time!
extraño!	How strange!
lástima!	What a shame!
le vaya bien!	Take care!
se alivie!	Get well!
suerte!	What luck!
importa!	So what!
triste!	How sad!
va!	Pshaw, go on!
asco!	How disgusting!

Embarrassed? Then go somewhere private and shut the door!

To learn even more one-liners, *listen carefully* and *ask* Spanish speakers what words and phrases mean! Repeat and practice alone until you *feel* prepared. Instead of writing these phrases, just memorize the sounds!

"Close Encounters"

If you've been paying attention, this will *not* be difficult. All you do is try to figure out what would be the best "natural" response. Write it only if you want to. Go ahead and use any of the words and phrases introduced so far.

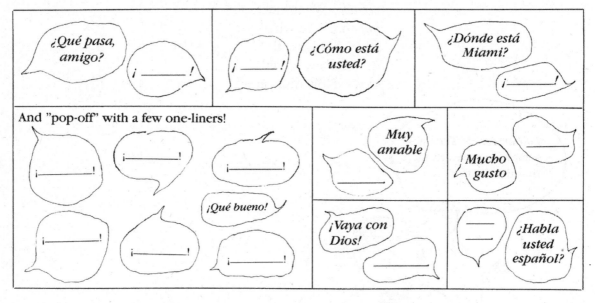

Try more than one response. Check any previous page for possible responses. And, just as you would do in an actual situation—be creative!

Fantastic *Frases*

For the bravest of babblers, here are some "advanced plays" that truly make folks sound like they know what they're talking about.

Por eso ...	Therefore ...	*A propósito* ...	By the way ...
O sea ...	In other words ...	*Al principio* ...	At first ...
Además ...	Besides ...	*Por lo menos* ...	At least ...
Por fin ...	At last ...	*Según* ...	According to ...
Por ejemplo ...	For example ...	*En general* ...	In general ...
Sobre todo ...	Above all ...	*Paso a paso* ...	Step by step ...
Sin embargo ...	However ...	*Poco a poco* ...	Little by little ...
En cuantoa ...	Regarding ...	*Sobra decir* ...	Needless to say ...

Here's an example of how it's done.

¿Mi carro? **En general,** *mi carro es excelente.*   My car? In general, my car is great.

Por ejemplo, *el color es perfecto.*   For example, the color is perfect.

Además, *es muy grande.*   Besides, it's very big.

Sin embargo, *el motor no es bueno.*   However, the engine isn't any good.

¿Mi carro? No sé.   My car? I don't know.

Now, you try one:

_____

_____

_____

Tengo una Pregunta
(I Have a Question)

Suggestions for Success

Try to apply the following suggestions when making questions and giving answers in Spanish.

- **Focus on the first word!** There are only a few "question words," so learn them. The next step is to listen for main words in the question that you can recognize or "guess at." Concentrate on the "topic" of conversation.

- **Answer as briefly as possible!** Take your time. And if you want, repeat the question you've been asked. At first, only respond with key words and short phrases.

- **Relax and remember your English!** Whether you're asking or answering, try using each word just as you would in English. Again, it's OK to mix both languages if you should forget!

The Primary *Preguntas* in *Español*

Make *muy* sure you can both understand and say the lifesaving *pregunta* words that follow:

¿*Cuál?* What/Which?
¿*Cómo?* How?
¿*Qué?* What?
¿*Dónde?* Where?
¿*Cuánto?* How much?
¿*Cuántos?* How many?
¿*Cuándo?* When?
¿*Quién?* Who?

HOT TIPS!

- All the *pregunta* words need accent marks. A few change meaning when you drop the accent: *como* (I eat) and *que* (that).
- Always put a "¿" at the beginning of a question, as well as the "?" at the end. ¿**De acuerdo?**

¿*Cuál ...?* (What or which ...?)

Let's begin with the *cuál* questions; which can sometimes be answered with one or two words. Here are the most common questions needed to get basic information. Notice how ¿*Cuál es su ...?* means What is your ...?

¿*Cuál* es su nombre?* What's your name? *Mi nombre es Juan.*
¿*Cuál* es su dirección?* What's your address? *Mi dirección es 363 Main St.*
¿*Cuál* es su número de teléfono?* What's your phone number? *Mi número es 555-1234.*
¿*Cuál* es su lugar de nacimiento?* What's your place of birth? *Mi lugar de nacimiento es La Habana.*
¿*Cuál* es su correo electrónico?* What's your email? *Mi correo electrónico es gringo@gringo.com.*

¿*Cuál* es su libro?* Which (one) is your book?
¿*Cuál* es su lápiz?* Which (one) is your pencil?
¿*Cuál* es su cuaderno?* Which (one) is your notebook?

- ¿*Cuál?* all by itself means, "Which one?" ¿*Cuáles?* means "Which ones" and is the word for "which" when there are *more than one.*

Make your own.

Nombre News (Juan, José, López, Pérez)

Keep in mind the following when you ask for a person's name.
- *¿Cómo se llama?* is another way to ask "What's your name?"
- *Primer nombre* is "first name."
- *Apellido* is "last name."
- *Me llamo* is "My name is ..."

Juan   José
Primer nombre
(Not all Hispanic people have two first names!)

López
Apellido paterno
(Dad's)

Pérez
Apellido materno
(Mom's)

NOTES
- In the United States, this guy is just *Juan López.*
- When a woman marries, she keeps her dad's last name, followed by her husband's.
- There's no "middle name" as we know it.

HOT TIPS!

- **Slow down,** relax! Ask your questions and give your answers *palabra por palabra* (word by word), *letra por letra* (letter by letter), or *número por número* (number by number).
- *Su* means "his," "her," or "its" in addition to "your." SO POINT!
- *Qué* can also be used to mean, How ...! *¡Qué grande!* How big!

¿Cómo?

All alone, *¿Cómo?* means *"What?"* or "How's that?" Use it like "How?" The classic *¿Cómo se llama?* literally means. "How are you called?" Now, can you tackle these other *cómo* concepts?

- *¿Cómo se dice?*   How do you say it?
- *¿Cómo se escribe?*   How do you write it?
- *¿Cómo está?*   How are you?

¿Qué?

¿Qué? always means "What?" as in *¿Qué pasa?* (What's happening?) Here are more *qué* classics:

Point to something and ask:
- *¿Qué es esto?*   What's this?

- *¿Qué es eso?*   What's that?
- *¿Qué son?*   What are they?
- *¿Qué significa?*   What does it mean?
- *¿Qué hora es?*   What time is it?

¿Dónde?

¿Dónde? is for direction; it is the "Where?" word. Whether you're looking for a person, place, or thing, just fill in the blank:

¿Dónde está   (Where's) ___?
"Look for" these phrases also:

¿Dónde vive?   Where do you live?

¿Dónde trabaja?   Where do you work?

¿Adónde va?   Where are you going?

¿De **dónde** es?   Where are you from?

¿Cuánto? and ¿Cuántos?

¿Cuánto(a)? (How much?) is the shopping word. *¿Cuántos(as)?* means "How many?" *Cuántos* applies to masculine nouns (*cuántos amigos*) and *cuántas* applies to feminine nouns (*cuántas amigas*). You can always "count" on these phrases:

¿Cuántos años tiene?   How old are you?

¿Cuánto tiempo?   How much time?

¿Cuánto cuesta?   How much does it cost?

¿Quién?

¿Quién es? means "Who is it?"

¿A **quién?** ...   To whom ...?

¿Quiénes son?   Who are they?

¿Para **quién?** ...   For whom ...?

¿De **quién?** ...   From whom ...?

NOTE
Words change a bit
when you want to refer
to *past* action. Don't be
concerned! For now,
use these as you would
one-liners:
¿Cuándo nació?
When were you born?
Fue ayer.   It was
yesterday.
¿Qué pasó?   What
happened?

¿Cuándo?

We'll be reading the clock and calendar soon, so let's warm up with some
¿Cuándo? quickies.

¿Cuándo …	*empieza?*	does it begin?
When …	*termina?*	does it end?
	llega?	does it arrive?
	sale?	does it leave?
	regresa?	does it return?

Long responses to these questions sound strange—so avoid using complex sentences. Keep those answers short!

¿Cuándo llega usted?—

Ayer.   Yesterday.
Hoy.   Today.
Mañana.   Tomorrow.
Por la mañana.   In the morning.
Por la tarde.   In the afternoon.
Por la noche.   At night.

HOT TIPS!

Remember:
• *mañana* = tomorrow
• *la mañana* = morning
• *Mañana por
  la mañana* (Tomorrow
  morning)

If you feel that you've
had enough for now,
take a break! Walk
around, name things,
or try out new words
you've already learned.
I'll be here when you
get back!

Who's Who?

To really get going, you've got to know these important words, which can designate the **"who"** of a *quién(es)* question. FYI—the "informal" Spanish words for "you" are not included here:

Use these words as you do their English equivalents and don't forget to point.

Yo   **I**

Usted   **You**

Ella   **She**

Él   **He**

Ellos   **They**

Ustedes   **You guys**

Nosotros   **We**

HOT TIPS!

- The preceding *quién* words (subject pronouns) work wonderfully as one-word responses. Notice how they also "start you off" when expressing a complete message: *¿Quién es inteligente?—Ella es inteligente.* (Who is intelligent?—She is intelligent.)
- *Él, ella, ellos,* and *ellas* can refer to things as well as people: *Los libros, ¿dónde están ellos?* (The books, where are they?)
- "Grab onto" the first word in all questions, because they will make answering so much easier!

Note:

Ellas = "They," feminine;

Nosotras = "We," feminine.

Tú = "You," informal;

Vosotros = "You guys," informal.

Posesión (Possession)

mi *amigo*
my friend

su *amigo*
their, your, his, or her friend

nuestro *amigo*
our friend

De él ...
De nosotros ...
De ellas ...

Just add "s" to both words (possessive adjective and noun) when talking about more than one.

- *mis amigos*
- *sus amigos*
- *nuestros amigos*

> **NOTE**
> *tu* = your, informal

¿De quién es? (Whose is it?)

If someone (or something) "belongs to" someone else use **de** (of/from) to tell who the person is:

It's Maria's friend.

*Es el amigo **de** María.*

The *Posesión* Principles

- Don't forget the *El* and *La* Business:
  nuestra amiga   our friend

- Don't get possessive words (adjectives) mixed up with *quién* words (pronouns):
  Yo tengo *mi* carro.   I have **my** car.

- Try these possessive words once in a while:
  Es ...   mío.   mine.
  (It's)   *suyo.* yours, his, hers, *or* theirs.

- When you get stuck, escape with *de!*
  ¿Es él un amigo   de ... usted?   yours?
                      él?   his?
                      ella?   hers?
  Is he a friend **of** *ellos?*   theirs (masculine)?
                      ellas?   theirs (feminine)?
                      ustedes?   yours?

- Perhaps you haven't noticed, but sometimes *en español*, it's OK to drop the *quién* word! It's already understood who's involved.
  (yo) **Estoy** bien.   I'm fine.

- "Casual" Spanish is centered on the little word *tú*. It means "you," same as **usted**. However, while **usted** is used to address anybody *with respect*, *tú* is *informal* and is used with children, your family, or friends.

The Reversal Rule

In speaking Spanish, it is sometimes necessary to *think backwards!* For example, if you'd like to *describe* something, just *reverse* the order of the describing word (adjective) and that of what's being described (noun):

A lot of **good tacos**.
*Muchos **tacos buenos**.*

… The same goes for *posesión*, Spanish first tells what belongs, then to whom it belongs:
John's house.
*La **casa** de **Juan**.*

… As well as for giving addresses:
642 Broadway Avenue
Avenida Broadway 642

… In addition to some "action" words, which are sometimes reversed:
I like coffee.
Me gusta el café or *El café me gusta.*

… And many one-liners:
Not now!
¡Ahora no!

HOT TIPS!

- When you talk, try to recall the Once-and-for-All Rule and the *El* and *La* Business (feminine and masculine gender). But *don't let this slow you down.* Forgetting sometimes won't hurt anything!
- You'll probably encounter *muchos ejemplos más* (many more examples), but *fear not*—you'll catch on!

¡Entrevista!
(Interview!)

If you're truly serious about learning *español*, the *Entrevista* is for you. Here's how it works. Simply "prepare" three common questions and then write one in each top box to the right of the words *Los nombres* (names). See chart below. Next, go some place nearby where you can easily "interview" Spanish speakers. List their names under *Los nombres*. (To get their names, use Question 1.) *Fill in their responses* in the boxes to the right under each question.

Los nombres (Names)	*¿Cuál es su nombre?* (What's your name?)	*¿Cómo está usted?* (How are you?)	*¿De dónde es usted?* (Where are you from?)
José López	José	bien	Puerto Rico
María Sánchez			
Luis Pérez			

NOTE
- Use a clipboard!
- Here are a few places where you can practice:
- A Hispanic restaurant
- A family gathering or party
- A Hispanic foods market
- An English as a Second Language (ESL) class or school
- A Hispanic cultural celebration or holiday event
- A friendly Spanish-speaker willing to "chat" with you on the Internet

INFORMACIÓN IMPORTANTE

- The more Spanish you learn, the more "complex" your questions will become. No need to "force it" now.
- Spend time chatting with folks you interview. It's fun!
- Start slowly. Practice first with people you are familiar with.
- A three-question interview like this takes *less than 2 minutes* per person. "Too busy" is *no excuse!*
- If you should have trouble understanding, just have them "write-in" their own responses!
- Your approach should be friendly. Stop strangers with *"Disculpe."* ("Excuse me.") *"Estoy aprendiendo español."* ("I'm learning Spanish.") *"Quiero hacerle tres preguntas."* ("I want to ask you three questions.") *"Muchas gracias."* ("Thanks a lot.") Trust me. They'll *love* to help!

The *Super-preguntas*

¿Cuál? _____

¿Cómo? _____

¿Qué? _____

¿Dónde? _____

¿Cuántos? _____

¿Cuánto? _____

¿Quién? _____

¿Cuándo? _____

> Without checking, can you give the meanings of these basic question words?

The following are *más* than just survival questions—they're *super!*

¿Le gusta?   Do you* like it?

¿Entiende?   Do you* understand?

¿Quisiera?   Would you (he, she) like some?

¿Hay?   Is there … *or* Are there any?

¿Por qué?   Why? (*Porque*, without the accent and spacing is "Because")

¿Quiere?   Do you* want it?

¿Tiene?   Do you* have some?

¿Puede?   Can you (he, she) do it?

*Also: Does he *or* Does she.

¿Puede recordarlo? (Can You Remember It?)

Answer these questions with a Spanish word or phrase:

- *¿Cuál es su número de teléfono?*
- *¿Cómo se dice "good-bye, yesterday, today, tomorrow, how, where"?*
- *¿Dónde vive usted?*
- *¿Cuántos años tiene usted?*
- *¿Quién es su amigo y su amiga?*

4

CHAPTER *CUATRO*

Mucho más

(Much More)

Do You Know Your ABC's? *(El alfabeto)*

¿Cómo se escribe?

Once you get rolling, you'll find yourself asking people everywhere how to say things *en español*. At work, in public, or on the phone—learning words will simply be part of your everyday routine. Remember the following *preguntas?* Well, go ahead and use them to "pry."

    ¿Qué es esto?   What's this?
    ¿Cómo se dice?   How do you say it?
    ¿Qué significa?   What does it mean?

They're *importantes*, yet sometimes you'll have to ask folks to "write it for you." Here are two lines that may help:

    ¿Cómo se escribe?   How do you write it?
    ¿Cómo se deletrea?   How do you spell it?

Simply hand them a pen and ask for it *"Letra por letra, por favor."* ("Letter by letter, please.")

El alfabeto

First, the *easy* part:

1 You already know the Big Five—*a, e, i, o, u*—their names are just as they sound!

2 Well, these letters are "close" to English. Say them in both languages—now!

b (beh "larga" or "grande")   *n* (´eh-neh)
v (veh "corta" or "chica")   *p* (peh)
c (seh)   *q* (coo)
d (deh)   *r* (´eh-reh)
f (´eh-feh)   *s* (´eh-seh)
k (kah)   *t* (teh)
h (´ah-cheh)   *w* (veh ´doh-bleh)
l (´eh-leh)   *x* (´eh-kees)
m (´eh-meh)

3 And here we have the four Spanish letters most gringos have problems with:

g (heh) *j* (´ho-tah) *y* (ee-gree-´eh-gah) *z* (´seh-tah)

4 The alfabeto also has **four more "letters"** than ours. Three of them are spelled with two letters together. And one has a ~ on top!:

ch (cheh) *ll* (´eh-yeh) *rr* (´eh-rreh) *ñ* (´en-yeh)

5 *Muy bien.* Are you ready to read the *alfabeto* in order? (Go somewhere "private" and *sing* it!)

a, b, c, ch, d, e, f, g, h, i, j, k, l, ll,
m, n, ñ, o, p, q, r, rr, s, t, u, v, w, x, y, z.

HOT TIPS!

- Spell *everything aloud* in Spanish from now on!
- But first, learn to spell your *nombre* and other *información de emergencia* (emergency information) just in case!
- Practice spelling over the *teléfono!*
- Use your online *Diccionario* or app often! And practice looking up words ALOUD!
- Try teaching *inglés* words to a Spanish-speaking person. You'll be forced to spell!
- As you learned from the Secrets to Soundmaking, "close" is good enough!
- "ll" and "ch" have been cut from the official Spanish alphabet. However, people do refer to them when spelling out a word.

Take a *Número* (Number)

0   1   2   3   4   5   6   7   8   9

If you don't know these numbers, go back to *"¡Viva el vocabulario!"* (page 23)

Sure, *los números* are easy. But do you realize how valuable they really are? In most cases, just by stating one digit at a time, you can save yourself *muchos problemas!*

¿Cuál es su ...

What is your ...

Go ahead, answer the following "personal information," *número por número:*

número de teléfono   (phone number)? _____

_____

número de seguro social   (social security number)? _____

_____

número de licencia de chofer   (driver's license number)? _____

_____

domicilio or *dirección*   (address)? _____

código postal   (zip code)? _____

código de área   (area code)? _____

número del apartamento   (apartment number)? _____

número de placa   (license plate number)? _____

número de tarjeta de crédito   (credit card number)? _____

_____

número del celular   (cell phone number)? _____

número de cuenta   (account number)? _____

You get the idea. Daily, practice saying aloud everything from your pocket change to passcodes to the TV channels. *Remember* that the trick is to keep it fun!

Take Some More Numbers

Let's begin by breaking down *los números* just as we did the Spanish *alfabeto*—it helps the memory. Use your own word-association system, and stay motivated by thinking of new and exciting ways you can use to practice *every day!*

1   First, some *weird* numbers:

10	*diez*	(dee-ehs´)
11	*once*	(ohn´-seh)
20	*veinte*	(veh-een´-teh)

> Practice these three until you can say them quickly and without *problemas!*

2   Next, the *easiest* ones:

12	*doce*	(Hear the *"dos"*?)
13	*trece*	(Hear the *"tres"*?)

3   Now, try to *picture these:*

14	*catorce*	(The number looks kind of "con**tor**ted")
15	*quince*	(Pronounced "Kings say")

4   And how about some *math?*

(10)	*diez y seis* (6) = (16)	*dieciséis*
	diez y siete = (17)	*diecisiete*
	diez y ocho = (18)	*dieciocho*
	diez y nueve = (19)	*diecinueve*

5   These multiples of *10* all end in—*nta*!:
Listen for the:

30	**trei**nta	(**tres**)
40	**cua**renta	(**cuatro**)
50	**cincu**enta	(**cinco**)
60	**ses**enta	(**seis**)
70	**set**enta	(**siete**)
80	**och**enta	(**ocho**)
90	**nov**enta	(**nueve**)

6   The numbers between are *all math problems!*:

(20)	*veinte y uno*	(1)	=	(21)	*veintiuno*
___	*veinte y dos*	___	=	(22)	*veintidós*
___	*veinte y tres*	___	=	(23)	*veintitrés*
___	_____	___	=	___	

NOTE
In Spanish, check out the difference in the numerical form of the ordinals:
1st = 1ª or 1°
2nd = 2ª or 2°
3rd = 3ª or 3°
… and so on.

NOTE
Three more "toughies":
500 = *quinientos*
700 = *setecientos*
900 = *novecientos*

NOTE
Primero and *tercero* lose their final letter when placed in front of masculine singular words:
Mi primer carro.
My first car.
Está en el tercer grado.
He is in third grade.

7   100 is *cien* (like, "**cen**tury").
101 is *ciento uno*.
201 is *dos cientos uno*.

8   1.000 is *mil* (like, "**mill**enium").
2.000 is *dos mil*, etc.
(Note that periods are used for thousands.)

9   **Order Up!**

1**st** *primera, – o* (*María es la primera. Juan no es el primero.*)
2**nd** *segunda, – o*
3**rd** *tercera, – o*
4**th** *cuarta, – o*
5**th** *quinta, – o*
6**th** *sexta, – o*
7**th** *séptima, – o*
8**th** *octava, – o*
9**th** *novena, – o*
10**th** *décima, – o*

Instant Time Telling

Learning to tell someone what time it is in Spanish will take *no time* at all! Although there are other optional ways to do it, this is clearly the easiest and fastest way to go:

¿Qué hora es?
What time is it?

Listen for *"hora"* which means "the hour."

¿Qué horas son? means the same thing.

... To answer, just look at your **reloj** (a watch or clock!) and give the **hora** followed by the **minutos**.

6:15
seis y *cuarto*

OTHER "TIMELY TIDBITS"

... in the **morning**   *de la mañana*
... in the **afternoon**   *de la tarde*
... in the **evening**, at **night**   *de la noche*
Noon   *mediodía*
Midnight   *medianoche*

If you want to say "**At** (a certain time)," say **A las ...**
at 6:15   "**a las** *seis y quince*"
Tiempo means "time, in general."
En punto means "on the dot."
Segundos are "seconds."

HOT TIPS!

- To tell time ... notice you only need to know 1–59.
- Have others teach you some other ways to tell time!
- Some folks say these to mean the same thing:
  – *de la tarde* ⎫
  – *por la tarde* ⎬ in the
  – *en la tarde* ⎭ afternoon

International Date Line

Still another practical use of *los números* is the yearly calendar. Let's begin with the most common words and phrases having to do with **el calendario** (the calendar):

el día   the day
el mes   the month
la semana   the week
el año   the year

¡El calendario!

los días de la semana

el lunes	Monday
el martes	Tuesday
el miércoles	Wednesday
el jueves	Thursday
el viernes	Friday
el sábado	Saturday
el domingo	Sunday

los meses del año

1 *enero*	5 *mayo*	9 *septiembre*
2 *febrero*	6 *junio*	10 *octubre*
3 *marzo*	7 *julio*	11 *noviembre*
4 *abril*	8 *agosto*	12 *diciembre*

¿Cuál es la fecha?   What's the date?

The year is always read as one large number:

2020 = *dos mil veinte*
(2000)   (20)

And whenever you give the date, apply the "Reversal Rule"!

June 3rd
el tres de junio

HOT TIPS!

- Ask *"calendario"* questions with *¿Qué?*, *¿Cuál?*, or *¿Cuántos?*
- **January** *(enero)* is the only month that doesn't "look like" *inglés!*
- Don't use *ordinal* numbers! Dates take cardinal numbers: 2 *(dos)*, 3 *(tres)*, etc. (Except for the **1st** … It's *el primero de: el primero de agosto* or *el 1° de agosto*.)
- To say "in July," it's simply *en julio*.
- What about CAPITAL LETTERS? *En español*, the months and days are **not** capitalized!
- On the "Spanish" calendar, *lunes* (Monday) is the first day of the week.
- *Miércoles* looks as strange as "Wednesday"!
- For *viernes*, think TG**IV**!
- *Sábado* and *Saturday* are close!
- "On Monday" is *el lunes*, but "on Mondays* is *los lunes*. Notice no "**on**."

CHOOSE 'n USE!

Los días
Hay una fiesta ...   There's a party ... (on Saturday, on Friday, etc.)
¿Trabaja usted ... ?   Do you work ...? (on Monday, etc.)
El programa empieza ...   The program begins ... (on Thursday, etc.)

Los meses
Ayer fue el ___ de ___.   Yesterday was the (20th, etc.) of ... (August, etc.)
Mi cumpleaños es en ...   My birthday is in ... (February, etc.)
¿Tiene usted las vacaciones en ...?   Do you have vacation in ...? (October, etc.)

Calendar Express!

Besides the basic calendar words it's nice to have other key words and expressions that will help get any date-line message across. As always, practice these *aloud* first, before you actually "go for it"!

The "*¿Qué día?*" questions:
- *¿Qué día es hoy?*   **What day** is today?
- *¿Qué día es mañana?*   **What day** is tomorrow?
- *¿Qué día fue ayer?*   **What day** was yesterday?
- *¿Qué día fue anteayer?*   **What day** was the day before yesterday?
- *¿Qué día es pasado mañana?*   **What day** is the day after tomorrow?

¡Las estaciones! (The Seasons!)
la primavera   spring
el otoño   fall
el verano   summer
el invierno   winter

*¿Cuál es **su** estación favorita?* _____. (Which is **your** favorite season?)

¡Más palabras importantes en el calendario!

HOT TIP!

Hay ("there is" or "there are") is a *muy* useful calendar word! *Hay* *una fiesta mañana!*"

el próximo   the next one
el pasado   the past one
actual   current
ahora   now; nowadays

el aniversario   anniversary
la cita   appointment
diario   daily
la fiesta   party
el fin de semana   weekend
el horario   schedule
la reunión   meeting
las vacaciones   vacation
el evento   event

How's the Weather?
(¿*Qué tiempo hace?*)

Making conversation with "weather chit-chat" is a *must* in any language and ¿*Qué tiempo hace?* is a question that's *excelente* as an ice-breaker. Then, you're bound to need these:

Hace ...

It's

frío	cold
calor	hot
viento	windy
sol	sunny
buen tiempo	nice weather

Está ...

It's

despejado	clear
nublado	cloudy
nevando	snowing
lloviendo	raining
lloviznando	drizzling

HOT TIPS!

• Here's the *easy way!*

  Hay ...
  There is
  or
  There are

neblina	fog
nubes	clouds
lluvia	rain
nieve	snow
humo	smoke

• If the *weather* is *not* moderate, use:

  ¡Hace mucho calor!
    It's very hot!
  ¡Hace mucho frío!
    It's very cold!
  nieva mucho
    It **snows** a lot
  llueve mucho
    It **rains** a lot

• *El clima* means "the climate."

Más Weather Words:

el agua	water	*el huracán*	hurricane
el aire	air	*la luna*	moon
el cielo	sky	*la marea*	tide
las estrellas	stars	*los relámpagos*	lightning
el fuego	fire	*el terremoto*	earthquake
los grados	degrees	*la tormenta*	storm
el hielo	ice	*el trueno*	thunder
la inundación	flood	*el tornado*	tornado

¿Puede recordarlo?
(Can You Remember It?)

- Count to one hundred by tens in Spanish.
- Give your birthdate in Spanish.
- In Spanish, tell what the weather is like today.
- Translate into Spanish:
  What time is it?
  What's the date?
  What's this?
  What's your address?
  It's snowing.
- Translate into English:
  ¿Cuál es su código de área?
  Hay doce meses en un año.
  ¿Cuáles son los días de la semana?
  ¿Trabaja usted mañana?
  La fiesta es hoy.

5

CHAPTER *CINCO*

Las personas

(People)

Es versus Está

*Are you totally confused about the uses of **es** and **está**?*

I say *es!*

I say *está!*

STOP THE FIGHT!
They're both right.

In Spanish, to say **is** or **you are**, it's **está** when referring to:
• **Location**   *¿Dónde **está** Carlos?—Él **está** allá!*
• **Condition**   *¿Cómo **está** Lupe?—Ella **está** muy bien.*
To indicate **"who"** or **"what" is**, use **es**:
*Usted **es** inteligente—Sí, pero, usted **es** más inteligente.*
*María **es** mexicana—No, ella **es** cubana.*

Notice the difference!
• ***Está***
   *Él **está** bien.*   He **is** fine.
   *La silla no **está** en la sala.*   The chair **is** not in the living room.
   *Ella **está** trabajando.*   She **is** working.
• ***Es***
   *El programa **es** importante.*   The program **is** important.
   *María **es** profesora.*   Maria **is** a professor.
   *¿**Es** usted puertorriqueña?*   **Are** you Puerto Rican?
That's all you get for now! All this stuff is further explained in Chapter *Siete*.

Get It Together—Part I

It's time to begin linking your *palabras* together! Strings of words bound by logic create meaningful messages. And remembering that pronunciation and grammar have little effect on communication allows us to "babble away" more freely. Another helpful trick to recall is that words can be joined in much the same order in Spanish as they are in *inglés!*

When we speak, *single words* and *one-liners* are the easiest ways to communicate our ideas:

> *¡Sí!*   Yes!
> *Él es.*   He is.

And adding words "to clarify" is *not* difficult:

> *¡Sí!, él es mi amigo.*   He is my friend.

Only, remember to use the "little linkers"—*y* (and), *o* (or), *pero* (but):

> *Él es mi amigo y ella es mi amiga, ...*
> *... ¡pero ella es más inteligente!*   ... **but** she is more intelligent!

Do you remember any of this stuff?

El libro de José   Jose's book
es azul y rojo,   is blue and red,
pero está en su casa.   but it's at his house.
¿Cómo se llama?   What's your name?
¿Y dónde vive?   And where do you live?
En diciembre, hay nubes y hace mucho frío, y llueve mucho.
In December, it's cloudy and very cold, and it rains a lot.

Moreover, don't worry about "getting stuck." Just plug in an English word. (Although the last option may elicit a wince or a laugh from your listener.)

> *Él es mi amigo y ella es mi amiga, pero ella es más inteligente y más* **rich!**

HOT TIPS!

- First, try *es* or *está*. Then, if your listener seems confused, smile and try it another way!
- In linking your Spanish words, recall and use these three concepts:
  1. The Reversal Rule
  2. The Once-and-for-all Rule
  3. The *El* and *La* Business
- Your Spanish pronunciation will improve the more you speak.

Un comentario about the *"tú"* form

Some readers might be wondering why I've continued to only mention the "formal" *usted* form, and not the *tú* or so-called informal form of *es* and *está*. Think about it. *Why bother?* It just becomes another thing GRINGOS have to worry about. Spanish-speaking people use the intimate *tú* when speaking to their friends. But that's because they can understand each other! And they're bound by cultural ties. My point here is simple. By following these shortcuts, tips and Secrets to Success, *you too* will be able to make friends and establish "informal" relationships with Spanish-speaking people. Soon your new pals will be teaching you the *tú* form, along with lots of other "inside info." Besides, the *usted* form is easier to remember and use. You'll find it's perfectly acceptable when speaking with *anyone!*

"How Ya Doin'?"

We've talked already briefly about the question: *¿Cómo está usted?* (How are you?) We know that the answer, *Muy bien* (Very well), is the old stand-by! Now let's check out the many other responses that tell folks **how you feel**.

(*Estoy and soy* can be used without ***yo!***)

If you want, try filling in the blanks:

Yo estoy _____. (feeling)
Yo soy _____. (personality)
(**I** am …)

fantástico(a) fantastic	*sorprendido(a)* surprised
bien well	*cansado(a)* tired
regular OK	*orgulloso(a)* proud
así-así not bad	*débil* weak
mal not well	*fuerte* strong
enfermo(a) sick	*dormido(a)* sleepy
feliz happy	*aburrido(a)* bored
triste sad	*ansioso(a)* anxious
ocupado(a) busy	*enojado(a)* angry
preocupado(a) worried	*confundido(a)* confused
nervioso(a) nervous	*emocionado(a)* excited

CHOOSE 'N USE!
* Estoy un poco …   I'm a little … (tired, sleepy, etc.).
* ¿Está usted muy …?   Are you very … (bored, anxious, etc.)?
* Carol está demasiado … y …   Carol is too … (sad, etc.) and … (worried).
* ¿Está … usted?   Are you … (surprised, etc.)?
* Es … él?   Is he a … (happy, excited, etc.) person?

HOT TIPS!

* With all the *palabras de descripción* (describing words), for emphasis, add:
  tan   so
  demasiado   too
  un poco   a little
  muy   very
  muchísimo   a whole lot
* Put two or three of these adjectives with *y* (and)!
* *Remember:* ***bueno*** means "good," ***bien*** means "well."

NOTE
Es and *está* change what you're trying to say about a person's condition:
*Él **está** nervioso.*   He is nervous.
*Él **es** nervioso.*   He's a nervous person.

¡Qué cuerpo!
(What a Body!)

It's time to learn the Spanish names for different parts of the human body. After all, people are made *de carne y hueso* (of flesh and bone):

la naríz
nose

el ojo
eye

el cabello
hair

la cara
the face

el cuello
neck

la boca
mouth

la oreja
ear

la mano
hand

el hombro
shoulder

el codo
elbow

el pecho
chest

el brazo
arm

la espalda
back

el estómago
stomach

los dedos de la mano
fingers

la pierna
leg

la rodilla
knee

los dedos del pie
toes

el pie
foot

¡Ayyy! (Ouch!)

Here are some Spanish words and phrases to help you express what may go wrong with the body.

el accidente accident		***Dolor de …***
la ambulancia ambulance		
la contusión bruise		*espalda* backache
la cortada cut		*muela* toothache
el dolor pain		*cabeza* headache
la emergencia emergency		*garganta* sore throat
la fiebre fever		*estómago* stomachache
la herida wound		
los primeros auxilios first aid		*Me duele.* It hurts.
la sangre blood		*Me siento mejor.* I feel better.
		Estoy malo(a). I'm ill.
		Estoy débil. I'm weak.
		Tengo resfriado. I have a cold.

Tengo resfriado de pecho.   I have a chest cold.
Tengo fiebre.   I have a fever.
Me duele el estómago.   My stomach hurts.
¿Hay dolor en el cuello?   Is there a pain in the neck?
¿Hay cortadas en los brazos?   Are there cuts on the arms?
¡Llame al doctor!   Call the doctor!

> **NOTE**
> Folks may use other body words:
> *la oreja* = el oído
> *el cabello* = el pelo
> *la cara* = el rostro

Más partes del cuerpo:

la piel skin		*la muñeca* wrist
el corazón heart		*el tobillo* ankle
la lengua tongue		*los dientes* teeth
el músculo muscle		*la garganta* throat
los pulmones lungs		*el pulgar* thumb
los nervios nerves		*la cadera* hip
los músculos muscles		

Family Ties

Without a doubt, one of your initial encounters in Spanish will eventually lead to speaking about family members. But before we take a look at *la familia*, let's first make an effort to master these *muy importante* "people" *palabras:*

el hombre   man
la mujer   woman
el niño   small boy
la niña   small girl
el muchacho   young boy
la muchacha   young girl
el bebé   baby
el adolescente   teenager
el señor or *Sr.*   a man or Mr.
la señora or *Sra.*   a lady or Mrs.
la señorita or *Srta.*   a young unmarried woman
la persona   person
el socio   partner
el amigo   friend
el enemigo   enemy
los compañeros   buddies
los amantes   lovers
el novio   boyfriend or groom
la novia   girlfriend or bride
los novios   sweethearts or bride and groom
damas y caballeros   ladies and gentlemen
los parientes   relatives
los hijos   sons or sons and daughters
los hermanos   brothers or brother and sister
los papás or *padres*   parents
los abuelos   grandparents

HOT TIPS!

- Make the necessary changes for feminine and masculine, according to the *El* and *La* Business.
- To make more sentences, go ahead and insert words from both of the following categories.
  ¿Quién? words:
  yo, usted, ella, él, ellos nosotros, ustedes.
  ¡Posesión! words:
  mi, mis, su, sus, nuestro, nuestros.

Ella *es* **mi** *amiga.*

Más "Persona" Palabras!
cualquier persona   anyone
todo el mundo   everybody
poca gente   a few people
mucha gente   a lot of people

CHOOSE 'N USE!

- *Lupe es …*   Lupe is … (my little girl, my friend, etc.).
- *… está aquí.*   The … (man, baby, etc.) is here.
- *¿Quién es …?*   Who is the … (person, enemy, etc.)?
- *¿Son sus …?*   Are they your … (relatives, grandparents, etc.)?
- *Me gustan sus …*   I like your … (parents, brothers, etc.).
- *¿Dónde están …?*   Where are (the) … (lovers, sweethearts, etc.)?

> **NOTE**
> *Los padrinos* are "godparents"—in most Spanish-speaking countries, the in-laws and godparents are considered important family members! *Los compadres* is the name parents and godparents of a child share.

Los miembros de la familia
(The Family Members)

Touch these pictures with your finger. Read aloud, and check for meanings!

Él He   **Ella** She

  Su   his, her, your, or their

Él es su esposo	*Ella es su esposa*
Él es su padre	*Ella es su madre*
Él es su hermano	*Ella es su hermana*
Él es su hijo	*Ella es su hija*
Él es su abuelo	*Ella es su abuela*

la sobrina	niece	*el sobrino*	nephew
el padre	father	*el yerno*	son-in-law
la madre	mother	*la nuera*	daughter-in-law
el abuelo	grandfather	*el cuñado*	brother-in-law
la abuela	grandmother	*la cuñada*	sister-in-law
el tío	uncle	*la hermana*	sister
la tía	aunt	*el hermano*	brother
el esposo or *el*		*el hijo*	son
marido	husband	*la hija*	daughter
la esposa	wife		
el suegro	father-in-law	*los nietos*	grandchildren
la suegra	mother-in-law	*los primos*	cousins

Familia **fine points:**

- The family unit is a vital part of Hispanic culture. Be sensitive.
- Other "terms of endearment" may be used besides the preceding words to name family members. Learn by asking or look them up in the dictionary if you need to.
- Notice how the informal *tú* is used for you instead of *usted* when family and friends talk to each other.
- Use *Es! Por ejemplo* (For example):

Es ... He's or She's
mayor   older
menor   younger
un(a) gemelo(a)   a twin
casado(a)   married
soltero(a)   single

Él (Ella) *es* ...
joven   young
viejo(a)   old
anciano(a)   very old

- Keep going:

la madrastra	stepmother
el padrastro	stepfather
la hijastra	stepdaughter
el hijastro	stepson

HOT TIP!

For affection, *-ita* and *-ito* can be added:
abuelita
hermanito
bebito

¿Puede recordarlo?
(Can You Remember It?)

- Name three different emotions.
- Name three different body parts.
- Name three different family members.

¡Mucho trabajo!
(A Lot of Work!)

Most folks don't spend all of their time "hanging around" the relatives at home. They go to work. Let's expand our "people-talk" to include the words needed to chat about work. Notice how most of these words refer to males only:

Los trabajadores (The workers)

el/la abogado(a) lawyer	*el/la enfermero(a)* nurse
el/la arquitecto(a) architect	*el/la estudiante* student
el/la asistente assistant	*el/la gerente* manager
el/la bombero(a) firefighter	*el/la ingeniero(a)* engineer
el/la cajero(a) cashier	*el/la jardinero(a)* gardener
el/la camarero(a) or *mesero(a)* waiter/waitress	*el/la jefe* boss
el/la camionero(a) truck driver	*el/la maestro(a)* teacher
el/la campesino(a) farmer	*el/la mecánico(a)* mechanic
el/la carpintero(a) carpenter	*el/la músico(a)* musician
el/la cliente client	*el/la pintor(a)* painter
el/la cocinero(a) chef	*el/la plomero(a)* plumber
el/la dentista dentist	*el/la policía* police officer
el/la dependiente clerk	*el/la secretario* secretary
el/la doctor(a) doctor	*el/la soldado* soldier
el/la dueño(a) owner	*el/la obrero(a)* factory worker
el/la empleado(a) employee	*el/la vendedor(a)* salesman
el/la empresario(a) employer	*el/la técnico(a)* technician
el/la taxista cab driver	*el/la ayudante* helper
	el/la cirujano(a) surgeon

Some more *profesiones:*

el/la payaso(a) clown
el/la astronauta astronaut
la actriz actress

el atleta athlete
el escritor writer
el/la agente agent

CHOOSE 'N USE!
- *¿Quién es …?* Who is (the) … (boss, chef, teacher, etc.)?
- *Quiere ser …* He/She wants to be a … (writer, farmer, lawyer, etc.).
- *… es excelente.* The … (painter, mechanic, actress, etc.) is excellent.

HOT TIPS!

- *¿Qué hace?* means "What do you do?" (also, What does *he* or *she* do?)
- Make sentences! Just put **Es** in front! (**Es** = he's, she's, you're.)
- *Sí*, these words **do** require the *El* and *La* Business, based on the worker's gender.

HOT TIPS!

- Use Spanglish! *El overtime; La happy hour; El break; El lonche.*

- Demand it!
  ¡Hable con el jefe!
    Talk to the boss!
  ¡Cambie su cheque!
    Cash your check!
  ¡Tráigame la lista!
    Bring me the list!
  ¡Haga su horario!
    Make your schedule!

- Request it!
  Yo quisiera …
  I would like …
  Yo quisiera un trabajo.
    I would like a job.
  un negocio.
    a business.
  mis vacaciones.
    my vacation.
  un seguro.   insurance.
  más beneficios.   more benefits.
  el éxito.   success.
  una oportunidad.
    an opportunity.
  un puesto.
    a position.
  una carrera.   a career.

- Threaten!
  ¡Voy a renunciar!
    I'm gonna quit!
  ¡Voy a salir!
    I'm gonna leave!

- Talk about him or her!
  Está …
  He's or She's …
  retirado(a)   retired
  contratado(a)   hired
  despedido(a)   fired

Trabajo, trabajo, trabajo …

There's really no way to present all the Spanish words related to *el trabajo* because we all hold different *trabajos*. The following is a *colección* of miscellaneous stuff. If you need to know the name of something specific at your workplace, ask a Spanish speaker for some help. (Remember: **¿Qué es esto en español?** is "What is this thing called in Spanish?")

Work on these words:

el sueldo	salary	*el horario*	schedule
la agencia	agency	*la huelga*	strike
el almacén	warehouse	*la junta*	meeting
el cheque	check	*la lista*	list
la cita	appointment	*la máquina*	machine
la computadora	computer	*el archivo*	file
la conferencia	conference	*el material*	material
el contrato	contract	*la oficina*	office
la copiadora	copier	*el producto*	product
el correo	mail	*el programa*	program
el entrenamiento	training	*la reparación*	repair
la entrevista	interview	*la tarjeta*	time card
la fábrica	factory	*la venta*	sale
los formularios	forms	*la impresora*	printer
la herramienta	tool	*la habilidad*	skill

CHOOSE 'N USE!

- *¿Dónde está …?*   Where's the … (factory, meeting, etc.)?
- *Hay problemas con …*   There are problems with the … (tool, machine, etc.).
- *Me gusta …*   I like the … (program, schedule, etc.).
- *Necesito mi …*   I need my … (check, contract, etc.).

The Good, the Bad, and the Ugly

Describing people in Spanish is no different from describing places and things. As you've discovered you can rely on the Reversal Rule! Whenever you want to add a *description*, simply think *backwards*.

*Él es un **hombre grande**.*

He is a **big man**.

> ### NOTE
> A different way to say the same thing is—*El hombre es grande*. And of course you'll need the *El* and *La* Business and the Once-and-for-All Rule:
> *Ell**as** son señori**tas** boni**tas**.* They are pretty girls.

Now, why not delve into these describers!

grande big	*feo(a)* ugly	*simpático(a)* nice
chico(a) small	*bonito(a)* pretty	*extraño(a)* strange
bueno(a) good	*guapo(a)* handsome	*fuerte* strong
malo(a) bad	*alto(a)* tall	*débil* weak
nuevo(a) new	*flaco(a)* thin	*largo(a)* long
viejo(a) old	*gordo(a)* fat	*bajo(a)* short in height
joven young		*corto(a)* short in length
perezoso(a) lazy		
trabajador(a) industrious		

Use these "little words" to elaborate:

más *grande.*   bigger
lo más *grande.*   biggest
tan *grande* **cómo ...**
   as big as ...

Él es
He's

- *un poco*   a little
- *muy*   very
- *demasiado*   too
- *tan*   so

lento.
slow.

Más Descripciones!

tonto(a)	dumb	*moreno(a)*	dark-haired
inteligente	smart	*pelirrojo(a)*	red-headed
brillante	bright	*calvo(a)*	bald
sucio(a)	dirty	*duro(a)*	hard
limpio(a)	clean	*blando(a)*	soft
lento(a)	slow	*rico(a)*	rich
rápido(a)	fast	*pobre*	poor
vacío(a)	empty	*valiente*	brave
lleno(a)	full	*cobarde*	cowardly
claro(a)	light	*interesante*	interesting
oscuro(a)	dark	*peligroso(a)*	dangerous
mayor	older	*roto(a)*	broken
menor	younger	*ancho(a)*	wide
fácil	easy	*estrecho(a)*	narrow
difícil	difficult	*suave*	smooth
barato(a)	inexpensive	*áspero(a)*	rough
caro(a)	expensive	*famoso(a)*	famous
frío(a)	cold	*equivocado(a)*	wrong
caliente	hot to touch	*disponible*	available
picante	hot to taste	*maravilloso(a)*	marvelous
rubio(a)	blond	*perdido(a)*	lost

CHOOSE 'N USE!

- *Marco no es ...*   Marco isn't ... (rich, bald, young, etc.).
- *Mi carro parece ...*   My car seems ... (full, slow, dirty, etc.).
- *Quiero algo ...*   I want something ... (dark, soft, etc.).
- *Usted no es muy ...*   You aren't very ... (fat, old, etc.).
- *Él es ..., ..., y ...*   He's ... (handsome, etc.), ..., (tall, etc.), and ... (nice).
- *¿Kim es ... o ...?*   Is Kim ... (lazy, etc.) or ... (industrious)?

6

CHAPTER *SEIS*

Las cosas

(Things)

"Mi casa es su casa"

As with all new words, it's best to learn these through "experience." Have a friend or another person command you to *move, point, pick up, carry,* or just *touch* the following common household objects:

Mueva ...
Move ...

Señale ...
Point to ...

Recoja ...
Pick up ...

Toque ...
Touch ...

Mire ...
Look at ...

Limpie ...
Clean ...

el sofá

el sillón

la lámpara

la silla

el televisor

el microondas

los cuadros

la mesa

la puerta

el teléfono

la tina

el librero

la chimenea

la cama

la estufa

el refrigerador

el excusado

el lavabo

el reloj

el tocador

CHOOSE 'N USE!
- *... está quebrado(a).*   The ... (lamp, refrigerator, etc.) is broken.
- *No puedo encontrar ...*   I can't find the ... (table, chair, etc.).
- *¿Cuánto cuesta ...?*   How much is the ... (computer, stove, etc.)?

¡Más cosas en la casa!
la alfombra   rug
la aspiradora   vacuum cleaner
los cajones   drawers
el cesto de basura   trash can
las cortinas   curtains
los gabinetes   cabinets
la lavadora   washer
la licuadora   blender
el ropero   closet
la secadora   dryer
el tostador   toaster
el trapeador   mop
los trastes   dishes
los cubiertos   silverware
la cafetera   coffee maker

¡Más aún (More still)
la almohada   pillow
el balde   bucket
la cobija   blanket
la escoba   broom
el espejo   mirror
el jabón   soap
la plancha   iron
la ducha   shower
la sábana   sheet
la toalla   towel
la esponja   sponge

CHOOSE 'N USE!
- *No tiene un/una ...*   It doesn't have a ... (cabinet, closet, etc.).
- *No me gusta el color de ...*   I don't like the color of the ... (rugs, curtains, etc.).

HOT TIP!

Lots of household objects can be said in English and are easier if left untranslated! (Discover more on your own!)

el switch
el microwave
los speakers

¿Dónde está?

Next time you can't find what you're looking for around *la casa*, send out a search party *en español!*

Here are a few places where it's most likely to be found.

Está en ...
It's in (on, *or* at) the ...

el dormitorio	bedroom	*el baño*	bathroom
las escaleras	stairs	*el césped*	grass, lawn
el sótano	basement	*la cocina*	kitchen
el pasillo	hallway	*el jardín*	garden
la sala	living room	*el garaje*	garage
el comedor	dining room	*el piso*	floor
el techo	roof	*el cuarto*	room
el desván	attic	*el apartamento*	apartment

Vocabulario especial

Voy a buscar ...
I'm going to look for (the) ...

No tengo ...
I don't have ...

¿Puede Ud. reparar ...?
Can you repair ...?

el aire acondicionado   air conditioning
las llaves   keys
la electricidad   electricity
los muebles   furniture
los enchufes   outlets
el portón   gate
la calefacción   heating
las cerraduras   locks
la tubería   plumbing
las luces   lights
la cerca   fence
el timbre   doorbell
las repisas   shelves

CHOOSE 'N USE!
- *Voy a revisar ...*   I'm going to check (the) ... (furniture, locks etc.).
- *No tengo un/una ...*   I don't have a ... (basement, attic, etc.).
- *¿Puede reparar ...?*   Can you repair ... (the plumbing, stairs, etc.)?

Las herramientas (Tools)
los alicates   pliers
el clavo   nail
el destornillador   screwdriver
la escalera   ladder
la manguera   hose
el martillo   hammer
la pala   shovel
el rastrillo   rake
el serrucho   saw
las tijeras   scissors
el tornillo   screw
la pintura   paint
la cinta   tape
la llave inglesa   wrench

Los materiales (Materials)
el alambre   wire
el asfalto   asphalt
la baldosa   floor tile
el cartón   cardboard
el cemento   cement
la goma   rubber
el ladrillo   brick
la madera   wood
la piedra   stone
el plástico   plastic
la tela   cloth

HOT TIP!

Try these wonderful
one-liners.
Se me perdió.   I lost it.
Se me olvidó.   I forgot it.
Se me quebró.   I broke it.

La vida en la ciudad grande
(Life in the big city)

Spanish fills our cities, … so let's leave the comfy confines of **la casa** and head into town. Walk, ride, or drive around *pointing* and *naming* things. (If you're caught talking to yourself, *don't stop!* It'll be too hard to explain.)

Los edificios (Buildings)
el almacén   warehouse, store
el banco   bank
la biblioteca   library
el cine   movie theater
el correo   post office
el departamento de bomberos   fire department
la escuela   school
la estación de policía   police station
la fábrica   factory
la farmacia   pharmacy
la gasolinera   gas station
el hospital   hospital
la iglesia   church
el museo   museum
la oficina   office
el restaurante   restaurant
el supermercado   supermarket
la tienda   store

Los lugares y sitios
(Places and sites)
el aeropuerto   airport
la acera   sidewalk
el barrio or *el vecindario*   neighborhood
la calle   street
el camino   road
la carretera   highway
el centro   downtown
la cuadra   city block
el ascensor   elevator
la esquina   corner
el metro   subway
el parque   park
el pueblo   town
el puente   bridge
el estacionamiento   parking lot
el centro comercial   mall

Keep looking around:
el semáforo   traffic light
el buzón   mailbox
la parada de autobús   bus stop

CHOOSE 'N USE!

- *¿Sabe dónde está …?*   Do you know where the … (museum, bank, etc.) is?
- *… está cerca de …*   The … (church, etc.) is near the … (school, etc.).
- *Espéreme Ud. en …*   Wait for me at the … (subway, corner, etc.).

La transportación
(Transportation)

el carro or *el coche*
or *el automóvil*

el helicóptero

la bicicleta

el camión

el barco

el avión

el autobús

el tren (train)
el metro (subway)

la motocicleta

el taxi

CHOOSE 'N USE!

- *¿Va por … o …?*   Are you going by … (taxi, etc.) or … (train, etc.)?
- *No me gusta viajar por …*   I don't like traveling by … (airplane, etc.).
- *Busco …*   I'm looking for the … (bus, etc.).

Más City Life
la piscina   pool
el rascacielos   skyscraper
el cementerio   cemetery
la cárcel   jail
la cantina   bar
las afueras   outskirts
el lote de carros   car lot
el zoológico   zoo
el campamento   campgrounds

There is a little piece of language—*ería*— (pronounced air-EE-ah) that is found *at the end* of words which name *stores* and *shops*. Watch the pattern!
la tortillería   tortilla factory
la mueblería   furniture store
la zapatería   shoe store
la carnicería   meat market
la joyería   jewelry store
la panadería   bakery
la peluquería   barber shop

As you travelers can see, the *ería* ending will work wonders for you as you're finding your way around *la ciudad grande*.

HOT TIPS!

• You may need these:
Las direcciones
N *(Norte)*
O *(Oeste)*
E *(Este)*
S *(Sur)*
• And fill out that form:
el condado
(county) _____
el estado
(state) _____
el país
(country) _____

Unas naciones y nacionalidades (Nations and nationalities)

Meeting people from many different parts of the world is becoming increasingly common. Here are some words to give your Spanish conversation an international flair.

España	Spain	*español(ola)*	Spanish
Francia	France	*francés(-esa)*	French
Los Estados Unidos	United States	*americano(a)*	American
(EEUU = USA)		*inglés(-esa)*	English
Inglaterra	England	*irlandés(-esa)*	Irish
Irlanda	Ireland	*japonés(-esa)*	Japanese
Japón	Japan	*chino(a)*	Chinese
China	China	*alemán(ana)*	German
Alemania	Germany	*italiano(a)*	Italian
Italia	Italy	*canadiense*	Canadian
Canadá	Canada		

- *Centroamérica*   Central America
- *Norteamérica*   North America
- *Sudamérica*   South America
- *Europa*   Europe
- *Oriente Medio*   Middle East
- *África*   Africa

Spanish Speaking Countries and Nationalities in Latin America

Can you find these on a map? Careful—they're all in Spanish!

la Argentina — argentino (a)
Bolivia — boliviano (a)
Chile — chileno (a)
Colombia — colombiano (a)
Costa Rica — costarricense
Cuba — cubano (a)
el Ecuador — ecuatoriano (a)
El Salvador — salvadoreño (a)
Guatemala — guatemalteco (a)
Honduras — hondureño (a)

México — mejicano
Nicaragua — nicaragüense
el Panamá — panameño (a)
el Paraguay — paraguayo (a)
el Perú — peruano (a)
Puerto Rico — puertorriqueño (a)
la República Dominicana — dominicano (a)
el Uruguay — uruguayo (a)
Venezuela — venezolano (a)

¡Razas! (Races)

Asiático(a)   Asian
Blanco(a)   White
Negro(a) o afroamericano   Black or African American
Indio(a) o amerindio(a)   Native American
Hispano(a)   Hispanic

CHOOSE 'N USE!
- *Me voy a mudar a ___.*   I'm moving to …
- *Está en la frontera de ___.*   It's on the border of …
- *¿Ha ido a___?*   Have you been to …

HOT TIPS!

- Unlike in English, nationalities are *not* capitalized!
- *La frontera* is "the border."
- *¿Adónde va Ud.?* Where are you going?
- *¡Voy a hacer un viaje!* I'm taking a trip!

Back to Nature

Let's get out of town for a while! But before we take off, why don't we "handle" a few of nature's little wonders that are within "reach"—right outside the door! And as we do with all new words of objects—let's *touch 'n talk*.

La naturaleza
(Nature)

el árbol	tree
el arbusto	bush
la arena	sand
la flor	flower
el pasto	grass
la hoja	leaf
el lodo	mud
el palo	stick
la piedra	rock
la planta	plant
el polvo	dust
la rama	branch
la semilla	seed
la tierra	dirt

Los insectos
(Insects)

la abeja	bee
la araña	spider
la hormiga	ant
la mosca	fly
el grillo	cricket
la avispa	wasp
el zancudo	mosquito
la cucaracha	cockroach

Los animales
(Animals)

Los domésticos
(the "domestic ones")
el caballo   horse
el chivo   goat
el gato   cat
la oveja   sheep
el pájaro   bird
el pato   duck
el perro   dog
el pez   fish
el pollo   chicken
el puerco   pig
el ratón   mouse
la vaca   cow
la tortuga   turtle
el conejo   rabbit

Los salvajes
(the "wild ones"):
el camello   camel
la cebra   zebra
el elefante   elephant
el hipopótamo
   hippopotamus
la jirafa   giraffe
el león   lion
el mono   monkey
el oso   bear
el rinoceronte
   rhinoceros
el tigre   tiger
el venado   deer
la víbora   snake
el lobo   wolf
el águila   eagle

Sometimes, animals aren't so easy to "handle," but have fun anyway!

CHOOSE 'N USE!

- *Hay ... allí.*   There's ... (a flower, a goat, etc.) over there.
- *¿Tiene ...?*   Does it have ... (bushes, chickens, etc.)?
- *No me gusta ...*   I don't like ... (mud, spiders, etc.).
- *¿Ha visto ...?*   Have you seen the ... (rock, camel, etc.)?
- *... es mi favorito(a).* The ... (tiger, tree, etc.) is my favorite.

- *... no es peligroso(a).* The ... (zebra, etc.) isn't dangerous.
- *... come mucho.* The ... (bear, lion, etc.) eats a lot.
- *... es inteligente.* The ... (monkey, dog, etc.) is smart.
- *... vive en la selva.* The ... (hippopotamus, etc.) lives in the jungle.

Now let our words head for

el campo
(the countryside):

el bosque   forest
el cerro   hill
la costa   coast
el desierto   desert
el lago   lake
el mar   sea
la montaña   mountain
la playa   beach
el arroyo   stream

el rancho   ranch
el río   river
la selva   jungle
el valle   valley
la cueva   cave
la finca   farm

CHOOSE 'N USE!

- *... es maravilloso(a).*   The ... (ranch, coast, etc.) is marvelous.

- *Ellos viven en ...*   They live in the ... (valley, ocean, etc.).
- *¡Vamos a ...!*   Let's go to the ... (lake, desert, etc.)!

"I'm Hungry" (*Tengo hambre*)

Food words, too, may differ slightly from *región* to *región*, but don't get nervous; instead, eat and ask! The words that follow can be used safely everywhere!

La comida
(Food!)

el *bistec*   steak
el *camarón*   shrimp
el *cangrejo*   crab
la *carne*   meat
el *cereal*   cereal
el *cerdo*   pork
el *dulce*   candy
la *ensalada*   salad
la *galleta*   cookie
la *goma de mascar*
   or el *chicle*   gum
la *hamburguesa*   burger
el *helado*   ice cream
el *huevo*   egg
el *arroz*   rice

el *jamón*   ham
la *langosta*   lobster
la *mantequilla*   butter
la *nuez*   nut
el *pan*   bread
el *pastel*   pie
el *pavo*   turkey
el *perro caliente*   hot dog
el *pescado*   fish
el *pollo*   chicken
el *queso*   cheese
la *salchicha*   sausage
la *sopa*   soup
la *torta*   cake
el *fideo*   noodle

> **NOTE**
> Try to "mumble" these words before you *dig in!*

Las frutas
(Fruit)

la *cereza*   cherry
la *fresa*   strawberry
el *limón*   lemon
la *manzana*   apple

la *naranja*   orange
el *plátano*   banana
la *toronja*   grapefruit
la *uva*   grape

el *melocotón*   peach
le *pera*   pear
la *piña*   pineapple
el *coco*   coconut

Los vegetales
(Vegetables)

la *cebolla*   onion
la *col* or el *repollo*
   cabbage
el *guisante* or *chícharo*
   pea

el *tomate*   tomato
la *lechuga*   lettuce
el *maíz*   corn
la *patata* or
   papa   potato

la *zanahoria*   carrot
los *frijoles*   beans
el *apio*   celery
la *espinaca*   spinach
el *pepino*   cucumber

La cocina
(Kitchen)

el abrelatas can opener	*la olla* pot	*el delantal* apron
el sartén frying pan	*la receta* recipe	*el mantel* tablecloth

CHOOSE 'N USE!
- *La ensalada tiene …*   The salad has … (carrots, onions, etc.).
- *¡ … es dulce!*   The … (corn, orange, etc.) is sweet!
- *No puedo comer …*   I can't eat … (lemons, strawberries, etc.).
- *¿Quisiera una … o …?*   Would you like a … (banana, etc.) or a … (grapefruit)?
- *… huele mal.*   The … (lettuce, etc.) smells bad.
- *¿Quiere …?*   Do you want a … (tablecloth, etc.)?
- *Voy a comprar …*   I'm going to buy a … (vase, etc.).

"Restaurante" Remarks

¡Qué …
How
deliciosa (or *sabrosa*)!
  delicious!
picante!   hot (to taste)!
caliente!   hot (to touch)!

Quisiera (I'd like) …
   or
Ella tiene (She has) …
   or
Tráigame (Bring me) …

algo de comer.   something to eat.
algo de beber.   something to drink.
el plato del día.   today's special.
el menú.   a menu.
más agua.   more water.
la cuenta.   the bill.
el postre.   the dessert.

¿Está …
Is it …
crudo(a)?   raw?
cocido(a)?   cooked?
frito(a)?   fried?
fresco(a)?   fresh?
maduro(a)?   ripe?
podrido(a)?   rotten?
hervido(a)?   boiled?

Now munch on these helpful tidbits:
Estoy en dieta.   I'm on a diet.
Para comer aquí.   To eat here.
Para llevar.   To go.
Quiero ordenar.   I want to order.
las comidas   The meals
el desayuno   breakfast
el almuerzo   lunch
la cena   dinner

Eat using these words:

la botella   bottle
la camarera or *mesera*   waitress
el camarero or *mesero*   waiter
el (la) cocinero(a)   cook
la cuchara   spoon
el cuchillo   knife
el platillo   saucer
el plato   plate
el pimentero   pepper shaker
la servilleta   napkin
la taza   cup
el tenedor   fork
el salero   salt shaker
el vaso   glass

Tengo sed

(I'm thirsty)
el batido   milk shake
la bebida   a drink
el café   coffee
el café descafeinado
    decaffeinated coffee
la cerveza   beer
el hielo   ice
el jugo   juice
la leche   milk
la limonada   lemonade
el refresco   soft drink
el té   tea
el vino   wine

Los sabores   *Los ingredientes*

(Flavors)	(Ingredients)	
Está ...	*el aceite* oil	*la harina* flour
It's ...	*el ajo* garlic	*la miel* honey
dulce. sweet.	*la canela* cinnamon	*la mostaza* mustard
amargo(a). bitter.	*el azúcar* sugar	*la pimienta* pepper
agrio(a). sour.	*el condimento* spice	*la sal* salt
seco(a). dry.	*la crema* cream	*la salsa* sauce
salado(a). salty.	*el vinagre* vinegar	*la vainilla* vanilla

CHOOSE 'N USE!

- *Necesito ...*   I need the ... (waiter, napkin, etc.).
- *... está sucio(a).*   The ... (glass, fork, etc.) is dirty.
- *Se me cayó ...*   I dropped the ... (spoon, cup, etc.).
- *Necesita más ...*   It needs more ... (sauce, mustard, etc.).
- *Hay demasiado(a) ...*   There's too much ... (salt, garlic, etc.).
- *No bebo ...*   I don't drink ... (wine, juice, etc.).
- *¿Quiere Ud. ... o ...?*   Do you want ... (coffee) or ... (tea)?
- *... está horrible.*   The ... (drink, etc.) is horrible.

HOT TIP!

Use *mucho* and *poco* for a **large** and **small** "amount." *Muchos* and *pocos* are for **many** and **a few**!

"What Are You Wearing?" (¿Qué lleva?)

… Get dressed in Spanish! The next time you're putting something on, name it *en español!*

NOTES

La ropa
(Clothing)
… *para mujeres*
    women's
… *para hombres*   men's
… *para niños*   children's

Clothing Commands!
- Take off your clothes!
  (*¡Quítese la ropa!*)
- Get dressed! (*¡Vístase!*)
- Put it on! (*¡Póngaselo!*)

el abrigo	overcoat
la bata de baño	bathrobe
la blusa	blouse
las botas	boots
las bragas	panties
la bufanda	scarf
los calcetines	socks
los calzoncillos	shorts
la camisa	shirt
la camiseta	T-shirt
la chaqueta	jacket
el cinturón	belt
la corbata	tie
la falda	skirt
la gorra	cap
los guantes	gloves
el impermeable	raincoat
las medias	stockings
los pantalones	pants
el pijama	pajamas
la ropa interior	underwear
el saco	sportscoat
el sombrero	hat
la sudadera	sweatshirt
el suéter	sweater
los tenis	tennis shoes
el traje	suit
el traje de baño	bathing suit
el vestido	dress
las zapatillas	slippers
los zapatos	shoes

Más cosas importantes:
el botón   button
el bolsillo   pocket
el cierre   zipper

CHOOSE 'N USE!
- *¿Dónde compró Ud. …?*
  Where did you buy the … (jacket, shirt, etc.)?
- *Me gusta el color de …*
  I like the color of the … (blouse, pants, etc.).
- *Necesito …*   I need the … (slippers, suit, etc.).
- *¿Cuánto cuesta …?*   How much is the … (dress, overcoat, etc.)?
- *… son muy viejos(as).*   The … (shoes, shorts, etc.) are very old.

Lavar la ropa
(Washing clothes)

"The cleaners" are *la lavandería*
"Dirty laundry" is *la ropa sucia*
"Detergent" is *el detergente*
"Stain" is *la mancha*
"Bleach" is *el blanqueador*
"Hangers" are *los ganchos*

HOT TIPS!
- Describe clothes with *los colores!*
- *Un par de* is "a pair of"
- You may hear *different words* used to name these things. *Who cares?* These will work fine!

¿Puede recordarlo? (Can You Remember It?)

In Spanish:
- Name three job titles.
- Name three descriptive words.
- Name three pieces of furniture.
- Name three rooms in the house.
- Name three buildings in the city.
- Name three plants or animals.
- Name three foods or beverages.
- Name three articles of clothing.

"Let's Go Shopping!"
(¡Vamos de compras!)

el dinero   money
el cheque   check
la tarjeta de crédito
   credit card

el cambio   change
la cuenta   bill
el cupón   coupon
el descuento   discount
el enganche   down payment
la ganga   bargain
la oferta   offer
el pago   payment
el precio   price
el recibo   receipt
la venta   sale
el débito   debit

La joyería
(Jewelry Store)

el anillo   ring
los aretes   earrings
el brazalete   bracelet
el broche   brooch
la cadena   chain
el collar   necklace

los diamantes   diamonds
las joyas   jewels
el oro   gold
las perlas   pearls
la plata   silver
el reloj   watch

Buyer's Babble!

¿Es todo?   Is that all?

¡Me gusta!   I like it!

¿Qué marca es?   What brand is it?

No me queda bien.   It doesn't fit.

Me quedo con esto.   I'll take this.

¿Cuánto cuesta? (or *¿Cuánto vale?*)   How much is it?

¿Cuánto pesa?   How much does it weigh?

Quiero probármelo(a,os,as).   I want to try it on.

Quiero cargarlo a mi cuenta.   I want to charge it (to my account).

¿En qué puedo servirle?   Can I help you?

¿Algo más?   Something else?

¿Cuánto por ciento?   What percent?

Es gratis.   It's free.

Necesito un dependiente.   I need a clerk.

Quiero un(a) cajero(a).   I want a cashier.

¿Cuál departamento?   Which department?

Unas Extras

la bolsa   bag; purse

la caja   box

la cartera   wallet

el cepillo   brush

la cinta   ribbon

la maleta   suitcase

el maletín   briefcase

el maquillaje   make-up

la mochila   knapsack

el paraguas   umbrella

el peine   comb

el perfume   perfume

el espejo   mirror

la canasta   basket

¿Cuál es su talla?
(What's your size?)

Uso un ...
I take a ...

chico(a)   small

mediano(a)   medium

grande   large

extra   X large

chiquito(a)   petite

CHOOSE 'N USE!

- *Busco ...*   I am looking for the ... (sale, perfume, etc.).
- *Quisiera ...*   I'd like the ... (receipt, change, etc.).
- *¿Se vende ...?*   Do you sell ... (rings, combs, etc.)?
- *¿Dónde están ...?*   Where are the ... (suitcases, diamonds, etc.)?

"Get into the Act!"

There's no better way to learn than by *doing*. That is why the best language programs include *commands* as a method to teach both *actions* as well as *objects*.

¡Cante la canción!
Sing the song!
¡Salude la bandera!
Salute the flag!

Commands involve both the speaker and the listener.

With friends and family, take turns giving each other *mandatos* (commands). Select common objects, and using the commands below, act them out! (They're great for work or play!)

Mueva (Move)	**la**
Lleve (Carry)	**televisión**
Levante (Raise)	(television)
Prenda (Turn on)	or
Traiga (Bring)	**esto**
Toque (Touch)	(this)
Señale (Point to)	or
Baje (Lower)	**eso**
Apague (Turn off)	(that)
Mire (Watch)	

¡Más mandatos!

Baile	Dance	*Firme*	Sign	*Regrese*	Return
Busque	Look for	*Lave*	Wash	*Repita*	Repeat
Cante	Sing	*Lea*	Read	*Saque*	Take out
Coma	Eat	*Limpie*	Clean	*Siga*	Continue
Compre	Buy	*Llame*	Call	*Suba*	Climb
Conteste	Answer	*Mande*	Send	*Tire*	Throw
Corra	Run	*Marque*	Dial	*Tome*	Drink
Escriba	Write	*Meta*	Put inside	*Vea*	See
Escuche	Listen	*Pida*	Ask for	*Venda*	Sell
Estudie	Study	*Quite*	Take away	*Venga*	Come

Let's make a *mandato!*

A simple approach to forming a command in Spanish requires knowledge of the three different action word (verb) endings. The endings are:

> **ar** as in *hablar*   to speak
> **er** as in *comer*   to eat
> **ir** as in *escribir*   to write

To make a *mandato*, drop the last two letters of the infinitive ("to") form and replace them as follows:

> **ar** → **e**
> *hablar* → *¡Hable!*   Speak!
>
> **er** → **a**
> *comer* → *¡Coma!*   Eat!
>
> **ir** → **a**
> *escribir* → *¡Escriba!*   Write!

But **beware!** Some verbs are weird and simply have to be memorized.

> *ir* → *¡Vaya!*   Go!
> *venir* → *¡Venga!*   Come!
> *decir* → *¡Diga!*   Speak!

HOT TIPS!

- Because commands are exchanged so often between friends, you may hear folks using the *tú* (or informal) form of the action words. Don't get excited. Here are a few common "informal" commands:
  ¡Ven!   Come here!
  ¡Vete!   Go away!
  ¡Dime!   Tell me!
  ¡Espérate!   Wait!
  ¡Cállate!   Shut up!
  ¡Llámame!   Call me!
- Use the previously listed commands for now, and don't worry about forming your own yet. You'll get the idea with practice!
- To tell someone *not* to do something, just put **no** in front of the command!
- When you can't remember the name of an object, use **esto** for "this thing" or **eso** for "that thing."
- You can always get your idea across by simply using the basic action (verb) form preceded by *favor de* (please).
  Favor de hablar.
  Please speak.
  Favor de seguir.
  Please continue.
- Start now by following these simple commands!
  ¡Toque el libro!
  Touch the book!
  ¡Escriba su nombre!
  Write your name!
  ¡Baile la salsa!
  Dance the *salsa!*

Los **Mighty** *Mandatos!*

Here are some common commands that are almost always given alone, and they work well *all by themselves!* (They are actually two words rolled into one.)

HOT TIPS!

- Remember—inside each command is an *action word!* (Using commands will help you learn the Spanish verbs.)
- As you "command" and "order folks around," *be nice!* Add *por favor* (please) and *gracias* (thanks). And *smile!*
- Watch out for those (accent) marks! That part of the word must be said louder!
- Don't try to figure out *se, lo, me,* and the other "little endings." You'll get their meanings as you speak more. So for now, practice each command as you did the one-liners.
- Pick one command to play with each day! They're best for commanding *one person only!* To tell a *group* to do something, add an *n* to the action word: *¡Señalen!* means "You guys, point!"

¡Acuéstese!   Lie down!
¡Agárrelo!(a,os,as)   Grab it!
¡Cálmese!   Calm down!
¡Créame!   Believe me!
¡Cúidese!   Take care of yourself!
¡Déjelo!(a,os,as)   Leave it alone!
¡Démelo!(a,os,as)   Give it to me!
¡Despiértese!   Wake up!

¡Dígame!   Tell me!
¡Espérese!   Wait!
¡Hágalo!(a,os,as)   Do it!
¡Levántese!   Stand up!
¡Párese!   Stop!
¡Pregúntele!   Ask him or her!
¡Recójalo!(a)   Pick it up!
¡Siéntese!   Sit down!
¡Vamos!   Let's go!

As you speak, help convey meaning through facial expressions and body language.

7

CHAPTER *SIETE*

¡Acción!

(Action!)

Un Anuncio Importante

You are about to enter the next level
of proficiency in Spanish.

Please read:

- This chapter introduces Spanish action words or verbs. Do not be afraid! There is no "conjugating." Instead, general suggestions are made, and *practical* action word lists are presented here. But you still have to pay attention. Believe it or not, this stuff is what *makes Spanish really work!*

- As always, *mistakes are good*, so don't hold back. Keep a positive attitude, and do the best you can. Don't worry about every word! Use only what you need.

NOTE
Spanish is easy! Most action words have the same base form. This means that all you have to do to understand action words is focus on the *first part* of the word. Here's how it works: First, take a typical action, like "to work" (*trabajar*). Now let's see what the base **trabaj**- can do!
¡Trabaj-en! (Work!)
¡Trabaj-aron! (They worked!)
¡Trabaj-amos! (We work!)
¡Trabaj-ando! (Working!)
¡Trabaj-aba! (I used to work!)
¡Trabaj-aría! (I would work!)

Basics in Action

There are only three action word endings. The basic word-forms (infinitives) end in *-ar, -er* or *-ir*. That's it. Action words can be used all by themselves. You won't always be correct, but people will still understand. To get "extensive training" in *action words* (verbs), buy a textbook, or take a class. But for simple communication, try to pick up on the vocabulary and tips that follow.

A Big Step Toward Fluency

Words and one-liners are great, if you like to keep things short. But to make a Spanish conversation last, sooner or later you'll need the "to be" verbs, *estar* and *ser* (**"The Big 8"**).

Remember: you can drop the *quién* words if you like.

Estar

It seems GRINGOS tend to pick up the following words right away:

Yo	**estoy**	I **am**
Usted		You **are**
Él	**está**	He **is**
Ella		She **is**
(Una cosa)		It **is**
Ustedes		You guys **are**
Ellos	**están**	They **are**
Ellas		They **are**
(Dos or *más cosas)*		They **are**
Nosotros(as)	**estamos**	We **are**

Chances are you're already using these action words! If not, here it is in capsule form: ***Estar*** can mean **am, is** or **are** when talking about:

Condition
¿Cómo **está** *usted?*
or
Location
¿Dónde **está** *María?*

See how all forms begin the same?
Est – *oy*
Est – *á*
Est – *án*
Est – *amos*

Knowing these **four** magic words will make the difference!

A closer look at *estar*

- *Estás* is used with *tú*. (It means "You are" among friends or family members.)
- *Esta* without the accent mark (´) means "This." *Ésta es una mesa.* This is a table.
- "Think" a bit before you use them. Put your words together just as you do in *inglés!*
  I **am** happy. → ***Yo estoy*** *contento.* (**condition**)
  The chair **is** over there. → *La silla* **está** *allí.* (**location**)
- Check back on "*Es* versus *Está*"!

Take *un momento* to read the next few pages with care!

Ser

The other "to be" word is **ser** and it's BIG-TIME!

See how weird it is! You'll just have to watch closely. Trust me. It's worth it!

soy   I'm
es   you're, he's, she's, it's
son   they're, you guys are
somos   we're

Instead of location or condition *ser* words relate to:

- *the time*
- *names*
- *origin*
- *occupation*
- *nationality*
- *description*

Check out these examples. You should be able to translate:

Soy Tony.   Es italiano.   Somos dentistas.

Es de oro.   Son amigos.

Son las dos.   Es grande.   Soy de Los Angeles.

Es de día.   Es una enchilada.

Son para Susana y Roberto.

To Be or Not To Be

Estar

For location and condition (at this moment).

Ser

For everything else!

¡Atención!

Look closely amigos—you've only got **eight words** to remember! and *they don't ever change.* Use this as a "study chart":

estoy   **soy**

está   **es**

están   **son**

estamos   **somos**

HOT TIPS!

- To ask questions, simply add question marks before and after. *María es bonita.* Mary is pretty. *¿María es bonita?* Is Mary pretty?
- Or, if you'd like, the subject in question can be moved to the end: *¿Es bonita María?* (Word order in Spanish won't really hurt the message.)
- The informal "you" form of *ser* is *eres.*

Notice the *difference!*

Estar
Yo **estoy aquí**.   I'm here.
Ella **está** *bien*.   She's fine.
Mis amigos **están** *ocupados*.   My friends are busy.
Nosotros **estamos** *trabajando*.   We're working.

Ser
Yo **soy** *Tony*.   I'm Tony.
Ella **es** *cubana*.   She's Cuban.
Mis amigos **son** *altos*.   My friends are tall.
Nosotros **somos** *dentistas*.   We're dentists.

DO IT NOW!

By fooling around with these ASAP, gringos can immediately begin sending complete messages. Back up a few pages and reread. You'll be amazed at how much better your Spanish will be!

TRY SOME!

1. *Tony* **está** *en la casa.*
2. *Ellos* **son** *inteligentes.*
3. *Yo* **estoy** *bien.*
4. **Somos** *cubanos.*
5. **Estamos** *muy contentos.*
6. **Soy** *el presidente.*
7. _____
8. _____
9. _____
10. _____

Just Say No!

What is truly *magnífico* about *español* is that there are so many shortcuts to success! As we've seen, to say *"not"* in Spanish, it's *no* big deal. Do *nothing* more than place a *no* in front of whatever you're trying to say.

> *La rata **es** muy grande.*
> *La rata **no es** muy grande.*

And *no* matter how complex the action, to say "not" just say, *no!*
> *Ella **no** quiere leer libros y escribir ejercicios.*
> (She does **not** want to read books and write exercises!)

Take a second to scan these **muy** useful *no-no's*:

No ...   *hay.*   There **isn't** or **aren't** any.
importa.   It's **not** important.
me interesa.   **I'm** not interested.
le haga caso.   **Don't** pay any attention.
me dí cuenta.   I **didn't** realize.
lo aguanto.   I **can't** stand it.
se preocupe.   **Don't** worry.
sabía.   I **didn't** know.
puede ser.   It **can't** be.
me gusta.   I **don't** like it.

Now, what can you learn about action words from these examples? That's right. The "o" ending refers to "I."

No puedo   I can't.
No tengo   I don't have ...
No veo   I can't see.
No necesito   I don't need ...

No quiero   I don't want ...
No recuerdo   I don't remember.
No encuentro   I can't find ...
No entiendo   I don't understand.

HOT TIP!

In Spanish, when answering questions, you need a **double no**: *¿Está Juan?*— ***No, no** está.* (Is John there? *No*, he is *not*.) For words like *nadie* (nobody), put ***No*** in front of the verb: ***No** está nadie.* (Nobody is here.)

Let's *Tengo!*

Here's another "power play" *en español*—and truly a *must* for the rookie. Whenever you'd like to talk about **who has** what, use the action word *tener* (to have).

tengo and *tiene* are great for requests and chit-chat.

> *¿Tiene cambio?*   Do you have change?
> *Tengo dos hermanos.*   I have two brothers.

Tenemos (**We** have) and *tienen* (**you guys** or **they** have) are also nice to know.

Remember: you can delete the *quién* words if you like.

TENER   to have

---

*Yo **tengo***	I **have**	*Ustedes*	
		Ellos	*tienen* You, They **have**
Usted		*Ellas*	
Ella	*tiene* You, He, She **has**		
Él		*Nosotros*	*tenemos* We **have**
		Nosotras	

TENER can also mean *to be* in the following situations:

Tengo la culpa.	I'm at fault.	*Tengo razón.*	I'm right.
Tengo hambre.	I'm hungry.	*Tengo frío.*	I'm cold.
Tengo sed.	I'm thirsty.	*Tengo calor.*	I'm hot.
Tengo miedo.	I'm scared.	*Tengo sueño.*	I'm sleepy.
Tengo suerte.	I'm in luck.	*Tengo 18 años.*	I'm 18 years old.

See how these make great one-liners. And they all work with the other forms of **TENER** just as well:

> *Tenemos miedo.*   We're scared.
> *¿Tiene frío?*   Are you cold?
> *Tienen hambre.*   They're hungry.

… Here you go! Make some of your own:

_____

_____

_____

"What Are You Doing?" (*¿Qué está haciendo?*)

Verbs in Spanish are usually learned in a predictable order. First, the commands are picked up along with the "to be" words, **ser** and **estar**. Second come the action words referring to "now!" (I call this the **"-ing"** or **-ndo** form.) It's the easiest form to remember and to use. All that's needed is an *acción* word. To say "talking" for example, simply change *hablar* (talk) to *hablando*:

$$hablar \quad \rightarrow \quad habla\textbf{ndo}$$
$$(\text{talk}) \qquad\qquad (\text{talk}\textbf{ing})$$

The **-ndo** replaces the **-r**. All Spanish action words end in **-r**, so the **-ndo** or **-ing** form is *muy simple!* Start with the "ar" verbs, because most infinitives end that way:

- *trabajar*   *trabaja***ndo**
  work   work**ing**

- *comprar*   *compra***ndo**
  buy   buy**ing**

- *manejar*   *maneja***ndo**
  drive   driv**ing**

And here's how they work. Just add the forms of "estar":

Estamos trabajando en el garaje.
We're working in the garage.

Estoy comiendo con mis amigos.
I'm eating with my friends.

NOTE
Some *acción* words end in **-er** or **-ir** so you have to change the ending to **-iendo** instead of **-ando**:
- *comer*   *comi***endo**
  eat   eating

- *escribir*   *escribi***endo**
  write   writing

HOT TIPS!

- Relax! All you need to remember is either **ando** or **iendo**.
- And to "complete" your message, just put the *estar* words in front: "Maria **is** working." becomes *María* **está** *trabajando*.

Onward with ...*ndo*

The key to *real* fluency is to acquire as many *acción words as* possible. Try "fooling around" with these words. First, "-ing" 'em with *-ando* or *-iendo!* Then use them to make statements.

correr (run)	*Ellos están corr**iendo**.*	They're running.
caminar (walk)	*Estoy camin**ando**.*	I'm walking.
salir (leave)	*El tren está sal**iendo**.*	The train is leaving.

abrir	open	*jugar*	play	*pagar*	pay
aprender	learn	*limpiar*	clean	*parar*	stop
beber	drink	*lavar*	wash	*poner*	put
besar	kiss	*llegar*	arrive	*tirar*	throw
cerrar	close	*llevar*	carry	*vender*	sell
empujar	push	*llorar*	cry	*viajar*	travel
jalar	pull	*mostrar*	show	*volver*	return

Ready, Set ...

At this stage of the guidebook, most of you have already started to race forward, constantly in search of *más palabras de acción*.

You have found that knowing how to use the *-ndo* form changes everything. After jabbering a couple of *acciones*, along with some *vocabulario básico*, you have begun to feel like a native speaker. However, before you volunteer as a tour guide, let's first take a look at a few more secrets to understanding those action words!

HOT TIPS!

- Many action words are *muy* easy to remember.
  flotar float
  plantar plant
  visitar visit
  controlar control
  And some are easier to learn combined with other words
  marcar el número dial the number
  llamar por teléfono call by phone
  mirar televisión watch TV
- **Be careful!** A few action words are not what they seem!
  pretender to court someone
  embarazar to impregnate
  And a few of these words change a little when you "-*ndo*."
  leer (read) becomes *leyendo* (reading)
  dormir (sleep) becomes *durmiendo* (sleeping)
  decir (say) becomes *diciendo* (saying)
- When "-*ndo*-ing," are you putting *estoy, está, están,* and *estamos* "in front"?

Beyond ...*ndo*

There's no way that beginning "Spanish-speakers" can pick up all the different action word forms right away. However, after the "-*ndo*'s," it is possible to "shortcut" your way through some of the other grammar junk.

Here is a *grupo* of goodies that will help! You can put these phrases **in front of** action word "infinitives."

Hay que (One must) …	*trabaj**ar**.* (work.)
Me gusta (I like) …	*com**er**.* (eat.)
Favor de (Please) …	*escrib**ir**.* (write.)
Tengo que (I have to) …	
Debo (I should) …	
Prefiero (I prefer to) …	
Necesito (I need to) …	
Puedo (I can) …	
Deseo (I wish to) …	
Quiero (I want to) …	
Quisiera (I'd like to) …	

HOT TIP!

You'll be hearing folks add -*ado* or -*ido* to action words instead of -*ndo*. Don't worry about it. It usually means that the action has been completed. *¿Entend**ido**? (Understood?) Remember:* Action word infinitives have only three basic endings, (-***ar**, -**er**,* and -***ir***).

Se

A small number of *palabras de acción* have **se** attached. Don't get excited! It simply means that the action is one that *we do to ourselves*. Here's how they work.

lavar is "to wash."

lavarse means "to wash oneself." To *"-ndo,"* say—*lavándose* (washing oneself).

Add *estar* and it's, *Él está lavándose*. (He's washing himself.) The NOTE below will help explain everything else.

NOTE
- To say "I'm doing it to myself," use *me*.
- To say "We're doing it to ourselves," use *nos*.

Check out some *más!*
- *acostarse*   lie down
  Nosotros estamos acostándonos.   We're ly**ing** down.
- *bañarse*   bathe oneself
  Ella está bañándose.   She's tak**ing a bath**.
- *cepillarse*   brush one's hair
  Yo estoy cepillándome.   I'm brush**ing** my hair.
- *levantarse*   raise oneself up
  Yo estoy levantándome.   I'm gett**ing** up.
- *peinarse*   comb one's hair
  Juan está peinándose.   John's comb**ing** his hair.
- *sentarse*   sit down
  Ellos están sentándose.   They're sitt**ing** down.·

Here's what all these words look like together!
lavarse   wash oneself

Estoy lavándome	*Está lavándose*
Están lavándose	*Estamos lavándonos*

CHOOSE 'N USE!
- *¿Quién está ...?*   Who is ... (bathing, standing up, etc.)?
- *Estoy ... ahora mismo.*   I am (lying down, etc.) right now.
- *Estamos ... y ...*   We are ... (combing) and ... (brushing our hair).

lo, la le, les, me, nos

Understanding these little pieces of Spanish is easier than using them correctly. So for now, here's what they mean *when used with* action words!

lo; la it
le you, him, her
les you guys, them
me me
nos us

Here's what they look like in normal conversation:

Me lo dijo.   He told it to me.
Lo tengo.   I have it.
Nos escribe.   He writes to us.
Pregúntele.   Ask him.
No les hablo.   I don't talk to them.

And notice how they usually require the "Reversal Rule"!

La   *La estoy limpiando.*   I am cleaning it.
Lo   *Juan lo está haciendo.*   Juan is doing it.
Le   *Le están escribiendo.*   They are writing you (or him, her).
Les   *Les estamos diciendo.*   We are telling them.
Me   *María me está besando.*   Maria is kissing me.
Nos   *Ella nos está enseñando.*   She is teaching us.

This is not easy. Even native Spanish speakers sometimes have problems with these little devils! But don't let them bother you—for now, just be aware of their general meaning and importance.

HOT TIPS!

- Some action words in the *se* category also change when you *"-ndo"!*
- Let's face it, *se* is strange and needs a little explanation. But *don't let it slow you down!* There are too few *se actions* to worry about.
- You'll also hear *te*, which is informal for "you."
  ¡Te amo!
  I love you!
- Go online and search "object pronouns" if you need more info.

Here are more of those practical, everyday *palabras de acción* you **really can use** all the time!

Don't forget!
-er, -ir = *iendo;*
-ar = *ando!*

adivinar	guess	*jugar*	play
ahorrar	save	*juntar*	join
amar	love	*montar*	ride
apostar	bet	*nadar*	swim
aprovechar	take advantage	*odiar*	hate
		olvidar	forget
arreglar	arrange	*perder*	lose
asistir	attend	*pesar*	weigh
bailar	dance	*pescar*	fish
buscar	look for	*platicar*	chat
cantar	sing	*prestar*	lend
celebrar	celebrate	*probar*	try
cocinar	cook	*quebrar*	break
contestar	answer	*quitar*	take away
cortar	cut	*recibir*	receive
dar	give	*renunciar*	quit
desarollar	develop	*reparar*	fix
descansar	rest	*sobrevivir*	survive
desear	wish	*soñar*	dream
disfrutar	enjoy	*subir*	climb
empezar	begin	*terminar*	finish
encontrar	find	*tocar*	touch
escuchar	listen	*traducir*	translate
evitar	avoid	*usar*	use
gastar	spend	*viajar*	travel
gritar	yell	*volar*	fly

HOT TIPS!

- It's very likely that you're going to hear many action words that *mean the same* as those listed here! Learn those, too— in case you're "in a bind."
- Some action words have two or more useful meanings: *ganar* (win, earn); *tomar* (take, drink); *hacer* (do, make); *pegar* (hit, stick); *dejar* (leave behind, allow); *pasar* (pass, happen).
- Most commonly used action words end in *-ar*, so use the "*-ando*'s" first!
- Don't worry about spellings now. Speak first!

CHOOSE 'N USE!

- *Mi amigo está …*   My friend is … (yelling, fishing, etc.).
- *Los niños están …*   The children are … (guessing, etc.).
- *Yo estoy … mucho.*   I am … (chatting, etc.) a lot.
- *Nosotros no estamos …*   We are not … (flying, riding, etc.).
- *¿Ustedes están …?* Are you guys … (listening)?
- *El Sr. Gómez está … y …*   Mr. Gomez is … (swimming) and … (climbing).

Las Acciones Locas

No doubt you have some questions about a few action words that don't seem to perform like the others. I call them *"las locas"* (the "crazies"). Let's take a look at a few of my favorites:

ir (to go)

What's *fantástico* about *ir* is that it tells:
- where you're **"going to"** and
- what you're **"going to"** do later

Learn these words:
Voy a (I'm "going to") … *México.*
Va a (You're, He's, She's "going to") … *mi casa.*
Van a (You guys, They are "going to") … *trabajar.*
Vamos a (We're "going to") … *comer.*

Saber and conocer (To know)

Saber and *conocer* both mean to know, but here's how they differ:
saber (sé, sabe, saben, sabemos) means "to know something."
conocer (conozco, conoce, conocen, conocemos) means "to know someone."

Yo sé mucho español.   I know a lot of Spanish.
Yo conozco a muchas personas.   I know a lot of people.

Each action word has four basic forms:
sé; conozco (I know)
sabe; conoce (you, he, she knows)
saben; conocen (they, you guys know)
sabemos; conocemos (we know)

HOT TIPS!

- Apply *ir a* to talk about the "future"! *¡Usted va a hablar español!* You're gonna speak Spanish! *¡María va a cocinar mañana!* Maria's gonna cook tomorrow! *¡Nosotros vamos a ir luego!* We're gonna go later!

- It might be a good idea to learn the *tú* or informal ways to say "you know."
  (saber) *sabes*
  Tú sabes hablar español.
  You know how to speak Spanish.
  (conocer) *conoces*
  ¿Tú conoces a María?
  Do **you know** Maria?

- Notice how you need to say **a** after *conocer* and many other action words when referring to people.

"What happened?"
(¿Qué pasó?)

There are tons more. Check out another Spanish program if you want to learn *más*!

Unfortunately, in Spanish, telling someone about previous events can be done several ways, depending upon your meaning. These are learned gradually when exposed consistently to lots of *español*. So, for the *momento*, let's view a few common "past" words that can help you ASAP!

> *Dijo*   said (you, he, she)
> *Fue*   went (you, he, she)
> *Comí*   ate (I)
> *Tenía*   used to have (I, you, he, she)
> *Iba*   was going (I, he, she); were going (you)

Estaba is used to talk about past action.
¿*Qué est**aba** haciendo?*   What *were* you doing?
Try these words:

Yo	*estaba*	I was
Usted	*estaba*	You were
Ella	*estaba*	She was
Él	*estaba*	He was
Ellos	*estaban*	They were
Ustedes	*estaban*	You guys were
Nosotros	*estábamos*	We were

CHOOSE 'N USE!

- ¿*Qué dijo …?*   What did _____ say? (Mary, Tom, etc.)?
- *Comí en …*   I ate at (the) … (restaurant, house, etc.).
- *No estaban …*   They weren't … (working, eating, etc.).
- *Él no tenía …*   He didn't have the … (name, number, etc.).
- *Fue a …*   He, She went to … (Japan, Europe, etc.).

Bueno, before we "*stop* the action," here's some helpful "inside info" on Spanish *acciones* y *actividades*.

- The worlds of Spanglish and slang have produced countless action words that can be heard daily, particularly in those areas of this country where lots of both Spanish and English are spoken. Try some! (Many sound the same in English.) And of course, *make sure you understand what you're saying*. Use your *best* judgment!

NOTE
- These go great with the *-ndo*'s. Also there are only three words to recall; not four!
- **Beware!** There are other **"was"** words.
- Believe me, this **"was" word** will get you going. You can finally start talking about the past!
  Ella estaba aquí ayer.
  She **was** here yesterday.
  Estábamos trabajando anoche.   We **were** working last night.
  Yo no estaba en casa.
  I **wasn't** home.
  ¿*Estaban jugando ellos?*   **Were** they playing?

- Read *español*. This is perhaps one of the best ways to learn the various action word forms (tenses). You'll soon be picking up and using stuff that used to take GRINGOS years to learn!

- Notice that action words in *español* have the same form for **we**! No matter what you're trying to say, the (*we*) ending is *-mos*.

	*so**mos**.*	**We** are.
Nosotros …	*baila**mos**.*	**We** dance.
	*comi**mos**.*	**We** ate.

The "you guys" or "they" ending is also easy to remember. Listen for the *n*.

Ellos …	*son.*	**They** are.
	*baila**n**.*	**They** dance.
Ustedes …	*comiero**n**.*	**You guys** ate.

These are only a couple of *muchos* patterns that remain consistent among Spanish action words. So pay attention! You are bound to discover many more.

- There's a unique set of words in Spanish that really go *bien* with the *palabras de acción*. They tell "**how** we do things." What's nice is they all end in *-mente*. (I call 'em the "-ly words." Notice how much they look like *inglés!*)

*breve**mente***	brief**ly**	*perfecta**mente***	perfect**ly**
*correcta**mente***	correct**ly**	*rápida**mente***	rapid**ly**
*efectiva**mente***	effective**ly**	*sincera**mente***	sincere**ly**
*inmediata**mente***	immediate**ly**	*usual**mente***	usual**ly**

And here's how they work:
*Juan está trabajando **rápidamente**.*   Juan's working rapidly.
*Estoy hablando **sinceramente**.*   I'm talking sincerely.
*Estamos jugando **perfectamente**.*   We're playing perfectly.
***Usualmente** no hay problemas.*   Usually, there aren't any problems.

¿Puede recordarlo?
(Can You Remember It?)

- Give a few commands in Spanish.
- Make three different statements using the word *estoy*.
- Make three different statements using the word *soy*.
- Ask a question using the word *tiene*.
- Make a statement using the word *hablando*.
- Name five basic verbs in Spanish.
- Make a statement using the word *estaba*.
- What does *perfectamente* mean?

8

CHAPTER *OCHO*

Los detalles

(Details)

Tell Me When!

We've become familiar with some of these "when" words already. But now—with our knowledge of *¿Cuándo?* (and some *palabras básicas*)—it's *time* to present the most popular words and phrases referring to time. (Recognize any of these one-liners?)

ahora   now; nowadays
ahorita   right now
a la madrugada   at dawn
a la puesta del sol   at sunset
anoche   last night
anteayer   the day before yesterday
antes   before
apenas   just
a veces   sometimes
ayer   yesterday
cada día   each day
casi nunca   seldom
después   afterward
entonces   then
esta noche   tonight
hace dos años   two years ago
hasta   until
hoy   today
luego   later

mañana   tomorrow
mañana por la mañana tomorrow morning
el mes pasado   last month
muchas veces   lots of times
nunca   never
pasado mañana   the day after tomorrow
pronto   soon
la próxima semana   next week
el próximo mes   next month
la semana pasada   last week
siempre   always
tarde   late
temprano   early
todavía   yet
todos los días   every day
una vez   once
un momento   a moment
un rato   awhile
ya   already

HOT TIPS!

- As with everything else, keep your eyes and ears open for *más!*
- *Tiempo* refers to "time in general." *La hora* is clock time. In some cases, *tiempo* can mean "weather."
- These "time" *palabras* are extremely valuable when used with your *action words!*

CHOOSE 'N USE!
- *Trabajo ...*   I work ... (today, always, etc.).
- *Estoy trabajando ...*   I'm working ... (right now, late, etc.).
- *Estaba trabajando ...*   I was working ... (yesterday, then, etc.).
- *He trabajado ...*   I've worked ... (before, every day, etc.).
- *Voy a trabajar ...*   I'm going to work ... (tomorrow, next month, etc.).

Tell Me Where!

Many "location" words were introduced earlier. The subsequent phrases and words allow us to express *exactly* where something (or someone) is located.

With these little beauties, you can answer almost any *¿Dónde?* question. They're OK alone, but they're better in sentences. (You'd be *lost* without them.)

abajo de down	*debajo de* under
adentro; dentro de inside	*desde* from
afuera; fuera de outside	*detrás de* behind
al fondo de at the bottom	*en* in, on, at
al lado de next to	*encima de* above
a lo largo de along	*enfrente de* in front of
alrededor de around	*entre* between
arriba de up	*hacia* towards
cerca de near	*lejos de* far from
contra against	*sobre* over

HOT TIPS!

- Create ways to practice these words with commands.
- *Acerca de* means "about" and shouldn't be confused with *cerca de* (near).
- *Reminder:* **estar** tells "where" in a sentence.

CHOOSE 'N USE!

- *Voy a ponerlo … las cajas.*   I'm going to put it … (inside, above, etc.) the boxes.
- *La oficina está … las tiendas.*   The office is … (near, next to, etc.) the stores.
- *El ratón está corriendo … ellos.*   The mouse is running … (toward, under, etc.) them.

Super "where" words!
cualquier parte	anywhere
por algún lugar	somewhere
por ningún lado	nowhere
por todas partes	everywhere

Here's how to "put together" these new words with others you've learned. (The word-joining process is a lot like that of *inglés*).
El sofá está **enfrente de** *la mesa.*   The sofa is in front of the table.

The Wimpy Wonder Words

Cosas grandes often come in small packages. In Spanish, there are a handful of tiny words which can be heard often because of their extreme importance. Combine one word from each column:

	mí (me)
	usted (you)
en (in, on, at) ...	*él* (him)
de (from, of) ...	*ella* (her)
a (to) ...	*ellos* (them)
para (for) ...	*ustedes* (you guys)
por (by, through) ...	*nosotros* (us)

_____(name of person, place, or thing)

And watch for these "Wee wonders!"

sin   without
con   with; check the changes:
- ***con****migo*   with me
- ***con****sigo*   with you, him, her, them
- ***con****tigo*   with you (between friends, family)

See how the *¿quién?* words change slightly when followed by "where" words!

HOT TIP!

Spanish has two "contractions": *a* and *de* always mesh with *el:*
del Soy **del** pueblo.   I'm **from** town.
al Voy **al** parque.   I'm going **to** the park.

Get It Together
—Part II

No more fooling around. It's time for the amateurs to step aside. This stuff is for the "pros" only!

Now that action words have been introduced, let's see what they look like when we combine them with all the other stuff. The key is to continue building strings of words—much like we do in English—but without fear of making mistakes!

Here's a simple formula:

La persona + *La acción* + *Lugar* + *Tiempo* = ¡*Mucho español!*
  person   action   place   time

Roberto está trabajando en la tienda ahorita.
 Robert is   working in the store right now.

To elaborate, add ***descripción*** and *detail!*

Mi amigo Roberto está trabajando en la tienda nueva hoy con María.
My friend Robert is working at the new store today with Maria.

Mis amigos americanos, Bob y Ed, no están trabajando mucho en la tienda nueva, porque ellos tienen clases todos los días.
My American friends, Bob and Ed, aren't working a lot at the new store, because they have classes every day.

Try mixing the order of your phrases.

Tengo el brazo quebrado y el sábado no puedo jugar en el parque con las otras muchachas.
I have a broken arm, and I can't play at the park with the other girls on Saturday.

Or, how about forming a *pregunta?*

¿Su hermana va a la tienda y va a comprar la comida para la cena y los dulces para los niños?
Is your sister going to the store and is she going to buy food for dinner and candy for the kids?

HOT TIPS!

- A "change" in the word order does not usually affect the meaning of the message!
- When you need to stop and "collect your thoughts," why not mutter a word, such as ¡*Momento!* (one moment)!

There isn't a thing you can't talk about!

Un elefante gordo estaba bañándose en el río ayer y estaba comiendo las plantas debajo del agua.
A fat elephant was bathing in the river yesterday and was eating the plants under the water.

When you get *bueno* at combining your Spanish words, the *el* and *la* Business, the Reversal Rule and the Once-and-for-all Rule will be applied without effort—automatically! Just remember, the more you "babble," the better you'll be!

Also, lengthen those commands! Check back on the *mandatos* and "add on" a few *palabras:*

¡Hable!   Speak!
¡Hable con María!   Speak with Mary!
… add some more:
¡Hable con María en la oficina!   Speak with Mary in the office!

And don't forget to combine two or more commands with the little linkers—*de, a, para, sin,* and *con:*
*¡Vaya a la escuela y **hable** con María en la oficina!*
Go to the school and **speak** with Mary in the office.

NOTE
Please say *Por favor.*

RSVP

As your strings of *palabras* get longer you'll need techniques to help you over any minor hurdles that may impede communication. Instead of walking away from a good conversation, try the RSVP (*R*epeat, *S*lur, *V*isualize, *P*ause) method of keeping things going. RSVP works, so master it *lo más pronto posible* (as soon as possible).

Repeat it!

- Repeating what you hear is still one of the best ways to acquire language while conversing. Hearing and saying (instead of doing nothing at all) new words more than once, make comprehension and speech that much easier. *¿Hay problema? ¡Sí … hay problema!*

Slur it!

- As ridiculous as it may seem, while you're learning Spanish, one very safe way to stay in a conversation is to slur and mumble those words, or parts of words, that you're not sure of. Using English, Spanglish, and even "creating" your own Spanish words are also very effective ways to reduce your "drop-out" rate.

Visualize it!

- When listening or speaking, just *picture* the unfamiliar words in their written form! Since Spanish is always pronounced exactly like it is spelled, comprehension is easy. Try it and you'll SEE!

And are you still using the other "visualization" technique? Keep playing those *word-picture* association games. Here are two of my favorites:
libro (book)   looks like *library*
cuartos (rooms)   looks like *quarters*

P-a-u-s-e it!

- For those moments of silence when you're desperately trying to recall words and form a response, try muttering these life savers!

… *a ver* …	Let's see …	… *este* …	Uh …
… *o sea* …	What I mean is …	… *bueno* …	OK …
… *es decir* …	That is to say …	… *pues* …	Well …

HOT TIP!

- Spanish mutterings are like those in English, so put two or three *in a row!* Well … let's see … OK! (*Pues … a ver … ¡bueno!*)

Not Much More to Fluency!

9

CHAPTER *NUEVE*

¡Bienvenidos!
(Welcome ... to the Majors!)

¿Quiere jugar? ("Wanna Play?")

Americans love sports and recreation. And so do many Spanish speakers worldwide. For the Latin American, soccer is the king of sports. (They call it *fútbol*.) *El béisbol* is popular as well; in fact, if you need "listening practice," many ball games are broadcasted on the internet, TV, and radio in both English and Spanish. As for individual hobbies (*pasatiempos*) in Latin America, they vary from person to person, just as they do in the United States. So, which of the following Spanish words might be helpful to you in *your* spare time?

Keep in mind, many sound like *inglés!*

el básquetbol	basketball
el béisbol	baseball
el boliche	bowling
el boxeo	boxing
el fútbol	soccer
el fútbol americano	football
el tenis	tennis
el vólibol	volleyball
el automovilismo	auto racing
el paseo en bote	boating
el ciclismo	biking
la caza	hunting
el buceo	scuba diving

el hockey; el surf; el golf; el badminton; el ráquetbol; el snowboarding; el rodeo
Guess their meaning!

And here are some action words in the games category:

correr	to run
esquiar	to ski
montár a caballo	to ride on horseback
navegar	to sail
patinar	to skate
pescar	to fish
acampar	to camp

CHOOSE 'N USE!

- *¿Le gusta … o …?*   Do you like … (baseball, etc.) or … (football, etc.)?
- *No sé mucho de …*   I don't know much about … (fishing, checkers, etc.).
- *… es excelente para su salud.*   … (Tennis, running, etc.) is great for your health.
- *Necesitamos …*   We need the … (net, ball, etc.).

HOT TIPS!

- Learn *más* from folks you play with!
- Find out what hobbies are common to folks in Spanish-speaking countries.

How about these "winners"!

¿Juega Ud. al tenis?   Do you play tennis?   *¿Cuántos tantos?*   What's the score?
¿Quién ganó?   Who won?   *¿Quién perdió?*   Who lost?

el atleta athlete	*el juego* game	*las pesas* weights
el campo field	*el partido* match	*el ejercicio* exercise
la cancha court	*la pelota* or *la bola* ball	*la canasta* basket
el entrenador coach	*la práctica* practice	*el guante* mitt
el equipo team	*la raqueta* racket	*el bate* bat
el estadio stadium	*la red* net	*el anfiteatro* arena
el gimnasio gymnasium	*el uniforme* uniform	*el campeonato* championship
		el fanático fan

*Mi **pasatiempo** favorito*   (My favorite **hobby**)

el ajedrez chess
el dibujo drawing
la fotografía photography
el juego de damas checkers
la lectura reading
los naipes or *las cartas* cards
el póker poker
el rompecabezas puzzle
escuchar música   to listen to music
mirar vídeos   to watch videos
usar la computadora   to use the computer
coleccionar collecting
la jardinería gardening
ir de compras shopping
los videojuegos video games
los artes marciales martial arts
el baile dancing
cantar singing

Jugar con los juguetes (Play with Toys)

Besides *los juegos* (games), we all grow up *jugando con* (playing with) toys. Kids of all ages will want to know the Spanish words for some of the common play *cosas!*

la bicicleta   bike
el tricicle   tricycle
la trotineta   scooter
los marcadores   markers
el animal de peluche
   stuffed animal
las caricaturas   cartoons
los chistes   jokes
los colores   crayons
la cometa   kite
los cubos   blocks
el disfraz   costume
la figura de acción   action toy
los fuegos   fireworks
el globo   balloon
la magia   magic
la muñeca   doll
los patines   skates
la patineta   skateboard
la pelota   ball
el rompecabezas   puzzle
los trucos   tricks

HOT TIP!

For a "toy" *object*, it's *tren de juguete* Toy train.

A theatrical play in Spanish has nothing to do with the word "play." It is an *obra de teatro* (a theater work). Yet, if *el drama* is your thing, maybe you can use these words below:

el ceño   frown
chistoso   funny
la comedia   comedy
la diversión   fun
las lágrimas   tears
la risa   laughter
la sonrisa   smile
la tragedia   tragedy

To play a musical instrument requires ***tocar*** (to touch) instead of *jugar*. Check out how *tocar* sounds when combined with these popular *instrumentos musicales* (musical instruments):

Toca ...
You play, He or She plays ...

Notice how many words look like inglés!

el piano	piano
el violín	violin
la guitarra	guitar
el saxofón or *el saxófono*	saxophone
la trompeta	trumpet
el tambor	drum
el clarinete	clarinet
el trombón	trombone
el órgano	organ
la armónica	harmonica
el arpa	harp
el oboe	oboe
la viola	viola
la flauta	flute

CHOOSE 'N USE!
- *Mi hijo quiere ...*   My kid wants ... (a guitar, etc.).
- *Tengo ... y ...*   I have ... (a piano, etc.) and ... (a violin, etc.).
- *¿Dónde puedo comprar ...?*   Where can I buy ... (a clarinet, etc.)?

Travel Treats!

We've already covered a few helpful areas for the traveler; such as transportation, shopping, and restaurant talk. The following collection of words, however, includes "the sweetest" of Spanish *palabras* and *frases*, which will assist not only the experienced *turista*, but the occasional vacationer as well. Let's begin with the "life-savers":

¿A qué distancia?   How far?
¿Cuál autobús?   Which bus?
¿Cuál calle?   Which street?
¿Cuánto tiempo?   How much time?
¿Está incluída(o)?   Is it included?
¿Está listo(a)?   Is it ready?
¿Está ocupada(o)?   Is it taken?
¿Hay agua potable?   Is there drinking water?
¿Puede ayudarme?   Can you help me?
¿Puede recomendar uno?   Can you recommend one?
¿Puedo pagar con esto?   Can I pay with this?
¿Puede repararlo?   Can you fix it?
¿Puedo tener cambio?   Can I have change?

And don't leave home, without …

Dónde está …?
Where's …?

NOTE
Use your time-telling skills!
- *¿Qué día es hoy?*
  What day is today?
- *¿A qué hora?*
  At what time?

la aduana   customs
el aeropuerto   the airport
el banco   the bank
el camino a …   the road to …
el centro   downtown
el correo   the post office
la estación   the station
el hospital   the hospital
el baño   the restroom
la entrada   the entrance

el hotel   the hotel
el mapa   the map
la parada de autobús   the bus stop
el restaurante   the restaurant
el semáforo   signal light
la señal   road sign
el teléfono   the phone
la tienda   the store
el estacionamiento   the parking
la salida   the exit

Unas personas necesarias
el/la criado(a)   maid
el/la dueño(a)   owner
el/la botones   bellboy
el/la conserje   concierge
el/la gerente   manager
el/la chofer   driver
el/la guía   guide

Here's a mixed bag of "Good 'n Plenty":

Quiero (I want) …
Necesito (I need) …
Quisiera (I'd like) …

> *darle propina* (to give you a tip)
> *hacer reservaciones* (to make reservations)
> *cargarlo(a)* (to charge it)
> *pagarlo(a)* (to pay it)
> *cambiarlo(a)* (to exchange it)
> *hacer una llamada* (to make a call)
> *ordenar* (to order)
> *un boleto* (a ticket)
> *la llave* (the key)
> *un taxi* (a taxi)
> *más toallas* (more towels)
> *una habitación* (a room)
> *más hielo* (more ice)
> *una bebida* (a drink)
> *la cuenta* (the bill)
> *un corte de pelo* (a haircut)
> *cancelarlo(a,os,as)* (cancel it)
> *uncuarto doble* (a double room)
> *el ascensor* (the elevator)
> *el servicio de cuarto* (room service)
> *el recibo* (the receipt)
> *irse de gira* (to go on a tour)
> *las escaleras* (the stairs)
> *la piscina* (the pool)
> *el gimnasio* (the gym)

NOTE
Pack these words away!
- *las maletas*   suitcases
- *la cámara*   camera
- *la visa*   visa
- *el pasaporte* passport
- *el seguro*   insurance
- *la agencia de viajes* travel agency
- *los puntos de interés* points of interest
- *boleto de ida y vuelta* round-trip ticket

… por favor!

El carro   (The car)

el aceite   oil
el agua   water
la batería   battery
la gasolina   gas
el motor   engine
la llanta desinflada   flat tire
¡Llénelo!   Fill it up!
la maletera   trunk
la capota   hood
los frenos   brakes

¡La pesca!   (Fishing)

el anzuelo   hook   *la salvavidas*   lifesaver   *el pescado*   fish
la bahía   bay   *la isla*   island   *el pescador*   fisherman
el bote   boat   *lanzar*   to cast   *pescar*   to fish
la caña   rod   *la marea*   tide   *la punta*   point
el carrete   reel   *el nudo*   knot   *la red*   net
el cordel   line   *las olas*   waves   *las rocas*   rocks

¡Márquelo y Suéltelo!   **Tag** it and **release** it!

Now, sample this selection! You might need them along the way:

el alfiler   pin   *la lata*   can
la bolsa   bag   *la medicina*   medicine
la botella   bottle   *las navajas*   razors
la caja   box   *el papel higiénico*   toilet paper
la cerradura   lock   *el periódico*   newspaper
el champú   shampoo   *la revista*   magazine
los cigarillos   cigarettes   *el sello*   stamp
el desodorante   deodorant   *el sobre*   envelope
el enjuague   conditioner   *la tarjeta postal*   postcard
los fósforos   matches   *la canasta*   basket
el hilo   thread   *el peine*   comb
el jabón   soap   *el cepillo*   brush
el maquillaje   makeup   *el cepillo de dientes*   toothbrush
las ligas   rubber bands   *la pasta de dientes*   toothpaste
la corta uñas   nail clippers
las pinzas   tweezers

El dinero

($) Find out the names for the currency and its rate of exchange before you travel anywhere.
Practice pronouncing the words and phrases you'll need for a few days before you leave!

Survival Signs

In traveling, the key to success is *awareness*. So keep your *ojos* open for these common *letreros* (signs) and you won't be "lost."

ABIERTO	Open	*EMPUJE*	Push
ADUANA	Customs	*ENTRADA*	Entrance
ALTO	Stop	*ESTACIONAMIENTO*	Parking
CEDA EL PASO	Yield	*GLORIETA*	Traffic Circle
CERRADO	Closed	*JALE*	Pull
CRUZ ROJA	Red Cross	*NO FUMAR*	No Smoking
DESCOMPUESTO	Out of Order	*SALIDA*	Exit
DESPACIO	Slow	*SANITARIOS*	Restrooms
DESVIACIÓN	Detour	*SE ALQUILA*	For Rent
DIRECCIÓN ÚNICA	One Way	*SE VENDE*	For Sale
EMERGENCIA	Emergency	*VÍA EQUIVOCADA*	Wrong Way

Las medidas (Measurements)

(Study your metrics!)	*onzas* ounces	*gramos* grams
el litro liter	*libras* pounds	*centímetros* centimeters
el metro meter	*pulgadas* inches	*peso* weight
el kilómetro = 5/8 mile	*tazas* cups	*longitud* length
el kilógramo = 2.2 lbs.	*millas* miles	*estatura* height
0°C = 32°F	*grados* degrees	*temperatura* temperature

And ask folks about any abbreviations you see!

CHOOSE 'N USE!

- *Primero vamos a buscar ...* First let's look for the ... (passport, bellhop, etc.).
- *¿Qué significa ...?* What does ... (customs, for rent, etc.) mean?
- *Présteme ...* Lend me the ... (camera, key, etc.).

What's in a *nombre?*

It's amazing how much influence Spanish has had over the years in many parts of the United States. Yet, we seldom stop to ponder the meaning of names of many of our cities, states, and landmarks. Some of them may surprise you.

Álamo (Poplar tree)	*Nevada* (Snowfall)
Amarillo (Yellow)	*Rio Grande* (Large river)
Colorado (Red)	*Sacramento* (Sacrament)
El Paso (The pass)	*San Antonio* (Saint Anthony)
Florida (Flowery)	*San Diego* (Saint James)
Las Vegas (The plains)	*San Francisco* (Saint Francis)
Los Angeles (The angels)	*Santa Fe* (Holy Faith)
Montana (Mountain)	*Sierra* (Mountain range)

Southwestern Specials

There's one part of the United States that's got *español* literally *everywhere!* Here are words that can be *seen* or *heard* throughout the Southwest:

agua (water)	*palo* (stick, stump)
arroyo (creek)	*playa* (beach)
costa (coast)	*puerto* (port)
loma (hill)	*real* (royal)
mar (sea)	*río* (river)
mira (look)	*santa* or *san* (saint)
misión (mission)	*valle* (valley)
monte (mountain)	*vista* (view)

- *avenida*   (Avenue)
- *calle*   (Street)

- *camino*   (Road)
- *del*   (of the)

And how about *los nombres de personas!* Obviously, those listed here are only the most prevalent. Yours may or may not have an equivalent. (*Ask around!*)

Male Names

Al   *(Alfredo)*
Bob   *(Roberto)*
Charlie   *(Carlos)*
Ed   *(Eduardo)*
Frank   *(Francisco)*
George   *(Jorge)*
Jim   *(Jaime)*
Joe   *(José)*
John   *(Juan)*
Mark   *(Marcos)*
Mike   *(Miguel)*
Peter   *(Pedro)*
Rick   *(Ricardo)*
Steve   *(Esteban)*
Tom   *(Tomás)*
William   *(Guillermo)*

Female Names

Alice   *(Alicia)*
Ann   *(Ana)*
Barb   *(Bárbara)*
Carol   *(Carolina)*
Debbie   *(Débora)*
Helen   *(Elena)*
Jane   *(Juanita)*
Kathy   *(Catalina)*
Liz   *(Isabel)*
Lynn   *(Lina)*
Marge   *(Margarita)*
Martha   *(Marta)*
Mary   *(María)*
Nancy   *(Anita)*
Sally   *(Sara)*
Susan   *(Susana)*

HOT TIPS!

- Some names are written the same in both languages: David, Samuel, Daniel, Gloria, Linda, Virginia.
- Some have "nicknames":
  Francisco   "Nacho"
  Guillermo   "Memo"
  José   "Pepe"
- And add **-*ito*** for endearment
  *Juan   "Juan**ito**"*

That's *Amor*

This guidebook would be incomplete without the presentation of the most significant Spanish "love lines." Romance is only a few *palabras* away.

Soy ...	*casado(a)*	married
I'm ...	*soltero(a)*	single
	divorciado(a)	divorced
	viudo(a)	widowed

"Power Lines"

Estoy enamorado(a).   I'm in love.
Es una promesa.   It's a promise.
¿Te gustó?   Did you enjoy it?
Me divertí mucho.   I had a nice time.
¿Puedo verte más tarde?   Can I see you later?
¿Quieres casarte conmigo?   Will you marry me?
¿Quisieras ...   Would you like to ...
   bailar? dance?
   dar un paseo? take a walk?
   platicar? chat?
   salir conmigo? go out with me?
Te quiero.   I love you.

¿Cómo es?   (What's he, or she, like?)

Es ...
He's or She's ...

agradable pleasant	*honesto(a)* honest
amistoso(a) friendly	*responsable* responsible
apasionado(a) passionate	*romántico(a)* romantic
aplicado(a) studious	*simpático(a)* nice
chistoso(a) funny	*sincero(a)* sincere
celoso(a) jealous	*tímido(a)* shy
cruel mean	
educado(a) well-mannered	• *besos.* kisses XXXX.
fiel faithful	• *abrazos.* hugs OOOO.
guapo(a) handsome	

Nice Things to Say

• Embrace these words!

HOT TIP!

Lovers and friends use the word *tú* for "you" instead of *usted*.

Girl to boy/Boy to girl:

chulo/a cute
mi amor my love
mi corazón sweetheart
mi dulce my sweet
mi tesoro my treasure
mi vida love of my life
querido/a darling
precioso/a precious

los amantes the lovers
el aniversario anniversary
la boda wedding
el cine movie
el concierto concert
la fiesta party
el matrimonio marriage
los novios the engaged
la pareja the couple

• A "date" is *una cita.*

Boy to girl only:

bella beautiful
hermosa lovely
linda very pretty
mi reina my queen
bonita pretty

CHOOSE 'N USE!

• *¡Él es tan ...!*   He is so ... (cute, romantic, etc.).
• *¡Sí! Pero es muy ... también.*   Yes, but he's very ... (shy, cruel, etc.) also.
• *Mi ..., te quiero tanto.*   My ... (darling, love, etc.), I love you so much.
• *Nos conocimos en ...*   We met at a ... (wedding, concert, etc.).

La religión, la política, y la filosofía

You can guess what *la religión, la política,* and *la filosofía* mean. And although it's better to avoid such controversial topics in any language, there's a chance they may pop up in beginning *conversación*. So if you're interested in the *argumento inevitable,* arm yourself with these fiery fundamental words:

Dios God	*el matrimonio* marriage
el capitalismo capitalism	*la justicia* justice
la cárcel jail	*la ley* law
el castigo punishment	*la libertad* freedom
el comunismo communism	*las mentiras* lies
el crimen crime	*el mundo* world
la cultura culture	*el partido* political party
la democracia democracy	*el pleito* lawsuit
los derechos rights	*el público* public
la economía economy	*el racismo* racism
la educación education	*la salud* health
la energía energy	*el tribunal* courtroom
el gobierno government	*la verdad* truth
el juicio trial	*la elección* election
los impuestos taxes	*la investigación con células madre* stem cell research

¡Muchos problemas!   (Many problems)

el aborto abortion	*la inmigración* immigration
las armas guns	*el medio ambiente* the environment
el cambio climático climate change	*las pandillas* gangs
el cáncer cancer	*el robo* robbery
la contaminación pollution	*la pobreza* poverty
las drogas drugs	*el abuso* abuse
la enfermedad sickness	*la obesidad* obesity
el estrés stress	*el SIDA* AIDS
el genocidio genocide	*los terroristas* terrorists
la guerra war	*la violencia* violence
la huelga strike	
la eutanasia euthanasia	

- *amar*   to love
- *odiar*   to hate

Yo creo …   ("I believe …")

el ángel   angel
la Biblia   Bible
los budistas   Buddhists
los católicos   Catholics
la creación   creation
los cristianos   Christians
el diablo   devil
Dios   God
el Espíritu Santo   Holy Spirit
Jesucristo   Jesus Christ
los judíos   Jews
los mormones   Mormons
el hinduismo   hinduism

los musulmanes   Moslems
los santos   saints
la Virgen   the Virgin
el alma   soul
el cielo   heaven
la fe   faith
el funeral   funeral
el infierno   hell
el milagro   miracle
la muerte   death
la vida   life
la salvación   salvation
los ateos   atheist

- *¿Qué piensa de …?*   What do you think of …?
- *En mi opinión …*   In my opinion …
- *Según …*   According to …

Whenever heavy topics are discussed, play it safe! Make *comentarios* with those "one-a-day" one-liners!

La cultura hispánica

Language and culture are inseparable. Therefore, it's imperative that we take time to look closely at the people who speak Spanish. Who are they? Where do they come from? What are their values, traditions, and life styles? Only through understanding one's *cultura* can true communication take place. Chatting is fine, but knowing where the speaker is "coming from" makes all the difference. So do a little research. Read up on Puerto Rican customs, Cuban society, or Mexican history. Learn by asking. Find out about family relationships, foods, and traditional holidays. And keep an open mind. Conversations always become more meaningful when there is mutual respect and consideration.

There's no way we can generalize and stereotype Spanish speakers. Folks from Cuba, Puerto Rico, and Mexico are not *all alike*. Sure, they share the same language, but each nation's heritage, diet, and everyday conversations differ in several ways. First, let's check out a few *diferencias*. These are considered popular among folks from Cuba, Puerto Rico, and Mexico:

Cuba

¡No chive!   Don't bother me!
¿Oigo?   Hello? (on phone)
¡Hola mi socio!   Hi, pal!
¡Concho!   Darn!
¡Oye chico, no seas patán!   Hey, don't be a jerk!
Zanjar un asunto.   To solve a problem.
Es un arroz con mango.   It's very complicated.
¡Qué pesado me cae!   I can't stand him!
¿Qué bolá?   What's up?
¡Qué guayaba!   What a lie!
¡Arranca!   Get going!

Puerto Rico

¡Oye, tocayo!   Hey, buddy!
No más.   Nothin' else.
¡Tranca la boca!   Shut up!
Ser la medio guayaba de …   To be …'s wife.
Saltar el charco.   Fly to New York.
¡Ay, bendito!   Dear Lord!
¡Arranca pa'lante!   Let's get going!
¿Me das pon?   Would you give me a ride?
¡Chévere!   Excellent!
¡A mi, plin!   I don't give a hoot!
¡A fuego!   That's really cool!
¡Ni pa!   No way!

Notice *how* they talk!

Mexico

¿Mande?   How's that?
¡Pásele!   Go ahead!
¿Bueno?   Hello? (on phone)
¡Ay, chihuahua!   Oh, my gosh!
¿Qué traes?   What's new?
¡Vámonos!   Let's go!
¡Dispensa!   Excuse me!
¡Derecho, derecho!   Straight ahead!
¡Qué gacho!   How mean!
¡Ándele!   Hurry up!
¡A poco!   Really!
¿Qué onda?   What's up?
¡No tengo feria!   I'm broke!
¡Eso que ni qué!   No doubt about it!

Unas palabras básicas ...

Cuba

blumers   underwear
espejuelos   glasses
fregar platos   wash dishes
gomas   tires
guagua   bus
haragán   lazy
jimagua   twin
maní   peanuts
mima   mom
mi viejo   my friend
pipo   dad
servicio   toilet
fajarse   to fight
playera   sleeveless T-shirt
pelado   penniless

Mexico

chamaco   kid
charreadas   rodeos
guacamole   avocado sauce
guajolote   turkey
huaraches   sandals
maíz   corn
mariaches   musicians
rancheras   ranch songs
sarape   blanket
tardeadas   afternoon parties
vaqueros   cowboys
chamarra   jacket
llanta ponchada   flat tire
tecolote   owl
gavacho   gringo

Puerto Rico

batey   front yard
bodega   grocery store
chino   orange
caucho   sofa
frisa   blanket
guineo   banana
melón   watermelon
negrito   loved one
papito   daddy
pelea de gallos   cockfight
sombrilla   umbrella
babilla   bravery
chavo   money
compai   pal
temporal   hurricane

Las comidas tradicionales (Traditional Foods)

Here are a few very popular dishes served throughout Mexico, Cuba, and Puerto Rico. *I recommend them all!*

Mexican Food
(Comida mexicana)

barbacoa (BBQ lamb)

birria (shredded goat meat)

bolillos (rolls)

buñuelos (deep fried donuts)

burrito (wrapped and filled flour tortilla)

carne asada (grilled beef strips)

carnitas (roast pork)

chile relleno (stuffed pepper)

enchiladas (usually cheese)

flan (vanilla pudding)

flautas (deep fried taco)

frijoles (beans, of course)

huevos rancheros (eggs with salsa)

lengua (cow's tongue)

menudo (tripe soup)

mole (chicken, turkey, or pork in sauce)

nopales (diced cactus)

pan dulce (Mexican pastry)

pozole (soup with pork)

quesadilla (cheese on tortillas)

sope (small, pizzalike tortilla)

taco (soft, not hard)

tamal (wrapped in corn husk)

tortillas (corn or flour)

tostada (flat and fried)

HOT TIP!

Ask "how" certain foods are eaten, or "how" they are prepared.

Cuban Food *(Comida cubana)*

ajiaco   (vegetable and meat soup)
arroz a la cubana   (white rice and fried egg)
arroz congrí   (rice with black beans)
arroz con leche   (rice, milk, and sugar)
arroz con pollo   (rice with chicken)
boniatos   (sweet potatoes)

chambarete   (lamb shanks)
empanada   (meat pie)
frijoles negros   (black beans)
malanga   (root vegetable)
mojito   (popular drink)
picadillo   (spicy hash)
ropa vieja   (shredded beef)
tostones   (banana chips)
yuca con mojo   (potatolike vegetable)

Puerto Rican Food *(Comida puertorriqueña)*

adobo   (meat marinade)
arañas   (shredded plantains)
arroz con gandules   (exotic rice and bean dish)
arroz guisado   (stew and rice)
arroz y habichuelas rojas   (rice and kidney beans)
bacalao   (pickled codfish)
camarones al ajillo (shrimp in butter sauce)

chayote relleno   (stuffed squash)
gandinga   (pork and kidney stew)
mofongo   (large fried green banana dish)
pasteles   (husk-wrapped dish)
quesito   (cream cheese pastry)
sofrito   (spicy seasoning)
vianda   (starchy vegetables)

¿Puede recordarlo? (Can You Remember It?)

- Name five words that tell "when?"
- Name five words that tell "where?"
- Name five words that relate to sports.
- Name three toys.
- Name five words you may need on a trip.
- Name three words that relate to love.
- Name five words that relate to religion, politics, or philosophy.
- What's you favorite Mexican food?

10

CHAPTER *DIEZ*

Las últimas palabras

(Last Words)

Talk About Language

Eventually, during the Spanish learning experience you will be forced to communicate with the "language" words commonly found in textbooks. (Remember these from English class?)

el adverbio	adverb	*la página*	page
el capítulo	chapter	*las palabras*	words
la conjugación	conjugation	*la práctica*	practice
el diálogo	dialog	*la pregunta*	question
el ejemplo	example	*el pronombre*	pronoun
el ejercicio	exercise	*la pronunciación*	pronunciation
la escritura	the writing	*el repaso*	review
la estructura	structure	*el símbolo*	symbol
el estudio	study	*el significado*	meaning
el examen	test	*el sonido*	sound
la frase	sentence	*el sujeto*	subject
la gramática	grammar	*el sustantivo*	noun
el habla	speech	*la tarea*	homework
el idioma	language	*el tema*	theme
la lección	lesson	*el tiempo*	tense
la lectura	the reading	*el verbo*	verb
la mayúscula	capital letter	*el vocabulario*	vocabulary
el método	the method	*la vocal*	vowel
la minúscula	lower case letter	*la voz*	voice

Things *you* might say:
- *¡El estudio de la gramática no es muy importante!*   The study of grammar is not very important!
- *¡Necesito más práctica y repaso!*   I need more practice and review!
- *¡No me gustan los exámenes y las tareas!*   I don't like tests and homework!
- *¡Comprendo el significado del vocabulario!*   I understand the meaning of the vocabulary!

Práctica, práctica, práctica (Practice!)

Traditionally, foreign language "practice" involved completion of grammar exercises, dialog memorization, and hours of audiolingual drills in a language lab. *Good News!* Practice techniques have changed—and in my opinion, for the better. The following methods are currently being applied worldwide in the most successful programs.

Learning Vocabulario

- Use the **command** words! Combine them with names of things you'd like to know. Use real objects or pictures of items. Have a friend "order you" to touch or move whatever it is you're learning.
- **Interview** Spanish speakers! List items like *sports* or *foods* and ask individuals which ones they like or dislike. Use a question like *¿Le gusta a Ud. …?* (Do you like …?) and check off their responses.
- Collect Spanish children's books, coloring books, or interactive toys. Since you're a "child" in the language, it's important to have lots of **visual exposure** to new words. While reading, point to each picture and "name it" in *español*. (This is really fun to do with the kids!)
- Make an audio digital recording. Ask a native Spanish speaker to read aloud a list of words that you need to know. Record different people, so you can hear all the different sounds. At first, don't bother with vocabulary you're not going to use every day. And offer to make an English recording in return!
- **Draw** pictures of items in special categories, and then **label** them. (The "unartistic," can find free pictures on the Internet!)

> **NOTE**
> Although it's not always feasible, these activities work better when learners are assisted by *native* Spanish speakers.

Comidas (Foods)

manzana   plátano   coco   melón

• **Be creative!** For example, practice descriptive words by downloading photos of either a strange-looking monster or your celebrity dream date!

muy gordo	*mucho dinero*
cuatro brazos	*muy bonita*
tres ojos	*muy inteligente*
orejas grandes	_____
_____	_____

La Computadora

Chances are your computer or smartphone will play a big part in your language learning experience. Not only is the Internet packed with free Spanish learning websites, but the number of free Spanish learning apps is on the rise! In Spanish, computer vocabulary is often the same as in English (*el email, la wifi, la internet, los apps, el streaming*, etc.). However, these other words might be useful, too:

Voy a ...	I'm going ...
archivar	to file
buscar	to search
conectar	to connect
descargar	to download
eliminar	to delete

encontrar	to find
enviar	to send
importar	to import
escoger	to select
guardar	to save
imprimir	to print
hacer "clic"	to click
recibir	to receive
reenviar	to forward
responder	to reply

¿Dónde está ...?	Where's (the) ...?
el adjunto	attachment
la basura	trash
el buscador	search engine
el buzón	mailbox
la contraseña	password
el correo electrónico	e-mail address
el mensaje	message
el menú	menu
el navegador	browser
la página inicial	home page
el programa	program
el servidor	server
el sitio web	website
el enlace	link
el ratón	mouse
la pantalla	screen
el teclado	keyboard
la barra de herramientas	tool bar

Check out the parts of an e-mail in Spanish!

Tony	**@**	**winner**	**.**	**provider**	**.**	**pe**
nombre del usuario	*arroba*	*nombre de dominio*	*punto*	*el proveedor de acceso a la internet*	*punto*	*el país*
(user name)	(at)	(domain name)	(dot)	(provider)	(dot)	(country)

Notice that *.com, .edu, .org*, etc. are not normal closings to an e-mail in other countries. In many cases, the country such as **.fr** (France), **.es** (Spain), and **.pe** (Peru) each have their own abbreviation.

Learning Basic *Conversaciones*

The best advice I can offer to those wanting experience in basic Spanish chit-chat is: *Just do it!* However, to "practice" conversation on your own, here are two helpful suggestions.

- A fun game one can play with any drawing program or app is to first create a few "characters," and then make up "foreign" responses which relate to the pictures. Use *any* Spanish words you know. (Write it in or just record something.)

- On a document, create a dialog of your own and then print it out— *one that you need* and will use often. With scissors, cut out each one-liner, phrase, and so on; then, mix them up. Practice putting the pieces in order so that it makes sense.

Bien, gracias. ¿Y usted?

Muchas gracias. Adiós.

José está en la oficina.

Bien. ¿Dónde está José?

Hola. ¿Cómo está?

De nada. Hasta luego.

Learning *Acciones*

Unquestionably, the most natural way to acquire verbs or "action words" is by having someone command you "to do something." In acting out the command, you "pick up" on the action word used. On the other hand, with **"visuals,"** you can begin to "talk" about what's going on. And creating your own "visuals" is easy. All you need are some paper, a printer, and access to free clip art on the Internet. Use the models given below, or develop your own. Get friends and family involved. Let that imagination run wild! Let's begin with a "visual" that helps teach the *affirmative*, *negative*, and *question* forms. Try these with *comiendo* (eating).

With a chart, we can expand on the action words. Be sure you begin with a column of people who represent *I*, *You*, *He*, *She*, *They*, and *We*.

The visuals can be "read":

a. *Yo **no** estoy comiendo manzanas.*
b. *Sí, ella está comiendo plátanos.*
c. *¿Ellos están comiendo naranjas?*
d. *¡Nosotros _____ _____ _____ _____!*

NOTE: Try searching for a fun visual game on your computer! Find graphics, invent situations, and apply all the vocabulary and verbs you've learned so far.

And this picture-story is for the superstar who already knows a bunch of action words. Go box to box, and tell what's happening in each picture. (When you get really *bueno en español*, you'll also be able to answer questions about the story, such as "What happened last night?" or "What happens every day?") You're not that far away.

Learning *"Grammar"*

> **NOTE**
> Children's books work very well for this activity.

As in all languages, in Spanish, grammar or "grammatical structure" is acquired "naturally" through trial and error. That's why a child's sentences always sound "so cute." It takes years of mistakes (and hours of classroom instruction) before anyone is able to respond consistently—using "proper grammar." Fortunately, for second-language learners there is a shortcut. Recent studies indicate that reading is one way to "fast and painless" language acquisition. Thus, by reading Spanish, learners can "pick up" basic rules of *la gramática española*. It seems that when GRINGOS read simple, interesting Spanish material regularly, their spoken Spanish improves—and their grammar usage becomes *correcto* most of the time!

The following is a brief story filled with the information introduced in Chapters 3 to 8. Before you read it, go back and skim the chapters. Then, read through the story. Next, check the chapters again to confirm comprehension.

Una historia (A Story)

Yo soy <u>Roberto</u>. Ahora estoy <u>muy bien</u>. Tengo <u>28</u> años y no tengo muchos problemas. Estoy trabajando para una <u>compañía</u> grande en los Estados Unidos con muchos de mis <u>amigos</u>. Me gusta mi trabajo. Me gusta mi familia, también. Todos son de <u>México</u>. En mi casa están mi <u>esposa</u>, mis <u>hijos</u>, mi <u>madre</u> y mi <u>abuelo</u>. La casa es grande. Tiene <u>cuatro</u> dormitorios, <u>tres</u> baños, una cocina <u>grande</u> y la sala. Pero no hay garaje. Es un problema porque tengo un carro <u>nuevo</u>. Es un Toyota <u>blanco</u>.

Mi esposa y mi madre están trabajando ahora en un <u>restaurante</u>. Están muy <u>contentas</u> allí. Mis hijos están estudiando en las escuelas públicas. Son muy inteligentes. Están estudiando el <u>inglés</u>. Mi abuelo no está trabajando porque tiene problemas con su <u>espalda</u>.

El <u>lunes</u> no voy a trabajar. Estoy preparando todo para un viaje a <u>México</u>. Cada <u>diciembre</u> toda la familia tiene una fiesta grande en nuestro pueblo. El pueblo está en <u>las montañas</u>, y es necesario comprar mucha <u>comida</u> y <u>ropa</u> especial. Por ahora estoy trabajando horas extra para pagar por el viaje.

Ahora estoy trabajando "overtime."

As you do Spanish readings like this, remember that open-ended techniques are used in stories to teach both grammar and vocabulary. Certain words are deleted, and readers insert any appropriate vocabulary. So "exchange" the underlined words for others! (The same could also be done with the action words!) Personal tales involving daily activities appear to work best.

HOT TIPS!

- Go to the Internet and click "Spanish language" instead of English. You will understand very little at first, but perseverance and imagination will get you far.

- Collect varied Spanish reading materials! In addition to *books, ebooks,* and *magazines*—gather inserts, labels, brochures, flyers, forms, posters, etc. (*Words with pictures* are best.)

- *Librerías* (bookstores), *bibliotecas* (libraries), *papelerías* (stationery stores), and *quioscos* (newsstands) sell or loan out literature for all reading levels. Many are found online. (Browsing in these places is nice—*you don't have to say a word!*)

- Avoid stopping to "study" words and sentences! Calmly skim over what you don't understand and try to focus on the main idea of each paragraph.

- At home, practice reading *aloud*. Record yourself, play it back, and then note any obvious "soundmaking" problems. (For best results, "read along" with native speakers!)

- Download a Spanish learning app on your smartphone or tablet today!

Unas preguntas para Ud. (Some Questions for You)

Here are 22 common *preguntas* you **should** now be able to answer. (*Por favor*, be brief!)

¿Cómo está usted?
¿Cómo se llama usted?
¿Cuál es su número de teléfono?
¿Quién es su doctor?
¿De quién es este libro?
¿Le gusta a usted la música clásica?
¿Qué hora es?
¿Qué día es hoy?
¿Qué tiempo hace?
¿Cuáles son tres partes del cuerpo?
¿Cuántas hermanas tiene usted?
¿Hay un perro en su casa?
¿Dónde trabaja usted?
¿Es muy bonita la Mona Lisa?
¿Dónde está su cama?
¿Es usted de los Estados Unidos?
¿Tiene usted hambre?
¿Cuántos años tiene usted?
¿Qué está haciendo usted?
¿Qué están haciendo los miembros de su familia?
¿Cuándo habla usted el español?
¿Qué hay detrás de usted?

The Answers?
...Write 'em
or
Just say 'em!
and
sorry, but you'll have to check 'em yourself!

Following are ten preguntas you **might** be able to answer!
¿Sabe usted mucho español?
¿Adónde va usted mañana?
¿Se lava usted las manos todos los días?
¿Quién fue el primer presidente de los Estados Unidos?
¿Dónde estaba usted anoche?
¿Quiere usted ir a Disneylandia?
¿Tiene usted miedo de los gatos negros?
¿Puede usted jugar al fútbol?
¿De dónde es usted?
¿Qué hace si ve el letrero "empuje"?

Before I Say *Adiós* ...

Without a doubt, this was the most difficult part of the entire guidebook to write. What more can I say? Everything you really need to get started in Spanish has already been introduced. (I know, because I once was in your *zapatos*.) Nevertheless, to make it all really work, I decided to summarize my thoughts in a series of closing remarks, personal comments and easy-to-follow suggestions which, when considered, lead gringo learners to immediate success in Spanish. *Por favor*, take heed.

Three Big Steps to *Comunicación*

NEXT:

Spanish for Gringos 2 … and beyond!

(mucho más vocabulario y gramática)
Third: You need to use the *"-ndo's"*

(más vocabulario y gramática)
Second: You've got to feel good about the verbs *Ser* and *Estar*.

(vocabulario y gramática)
First: You've got to know the *"Secrets to Soundmaking"*

Five Things to Always Keep In Mind

1   *Pronunciation* and *grammar* don't matter that much!
2   You don't have to speak until you feel like doing it!
3   Feeling comfortable around non-English speakers makes a difference!
4   You can't make any excuses for not learning!
5   Language learning takes place when you *relax* and have fun!

The Secrets to Success (All of these have already been mentioned. They are all **muy, muy importante!**)

- Try to be sensitive to and aware of cultural differences.
- Get in the habit of using Spanish *regularly*.
- Constantly memorize vocabulary through "word-picture" association.
- Experiment, take chances, and guess when you are unsure!
- Follow the practice tips and activities mentioned throughout *Spanish for Gringos.*
- *Add your own* ideas on how to practice and improve! This guidebook only establishes a base for your entire Spanish learning experience. Ask around, listen, and "build" from here.

Some *más* Advice:

- Try relaxation techniques before you "go for it." Stress-relief information is available everywhere.
- Don't "stop in the middle" to translate! Whenever you're listening, concentrate on the topic first, so that you have some idea of what's going on.
- Aggressive, outgoing, fun-loving Gringos usually learn Spanish faster than others. A childlike attitude also seems to help!
- When you are in an embarrassing situation, stuck, confused, or at a loss for Spanish words, rely on these for help: *Lo siento.* (I'm sorry.) *No recuerdo la palabra.* (I don't remember the word.) *Estoy estudiando español.* (I'm studying Spanish.)
- Please say *por favor.* In Spanish, you'll go far if you are courteous. The more respectful you are, the more Spanish you'll learn. So practice "polite" things to say. And as always—be sincere.
- Be patient! I know what the word "busy" means—but life's too short to pass up those rare opportunities to practice talking Spanish with someone. Trust me—take the extra moments *now* or later you'll regret not doing so.
- Some words mean *two* or *more* things in Spanish. Find out the appropriate use for each meaning. Dictionaries often help—but be careful! (It's always better to go *straight to the source*.)

NOTE

Do not memorize these rules! Simply be aware of the problems facing the beginner! Remember that "being close" is good enough. Besides, *all* of this stuff is picked up **muy rápido** once you actually get started.

HOT TIP!

- Memorizing jokes, tongue-twisters, rhymes, and folk song is a fantastic way to gain confidence wh learning language

- Spanish speakers of different countries don't all agree! It's not uncommon for them to "clash" over meanings of words, customs, or historical events. That's why it's important to be aware of the differences between Hispanic dialects. Try to be good at guessing where folks are from!

The Gringo Nightmares (*Problemas* we all seem to have!)

- **The Secrets to Soundmaking**   Even though pronunciation doesn't need to be practiced, becoming familiar with the "*Big Five* and the *Others*" will definitely make understanding and speaking a whole lot easier. (In particular, watch out for the *e, a,* and *i*!) Remember, in Spanish you *always pronounce the letters the same. There are no exceptions!*
- **The *EL* and *LA* Business**   Again, although it won't effect communication much, practice putting *la* in front of objects ending with *a*, and *el* before those ending with *o*. (You'll just have to remember which one goes with words *not* ending in *o* or *a*.)
- **The Reversal Rule**   When describing things, giving the date, or telling "whose," *think backward!* In these instances, the Spanish word order is "reversed."
- **The Once-and-for-All Rule**   Another pattern that should be mentioned is the way in which strings of words have to "agree" in Spanish. "Agreement" is best understood by observing some examples. Notice how the words "agree" with each other:

Los libros buenos   The good books

La muchacha bonita   The pretty girl

Muchas casas negras y blancas   Lots of black and white houses

¡Mini-problemas!

Here are a handful of **palabras** that always seem to bother the GRINGO learner. Pay close attention—they're "sneaky":

poquito   a little bit
pequeño   small in size

de nada   you're welcome
nada   nothing

muy   very
mucho   a lot

grande   big
largo   long

número   number
nombre   name

bueno   good
bien   well

que   that
qué   what

jueves   Thursday
huevos   eggs

dólar   dollar
dolor   pain

hombre   man
hambre   hunger

sí   yes
si   if

nuevo   new
nueve   nine

Add some of your own!

_____   _____

_____   _____

TEN MOST COMMON GRINGO PRONUNCIATION ERRORS

- Confusing the vowel sounds, such as hearing the "*i*" and thinking it's an "*e*."
- Confusing certain consonant sounds, such as hearing the "*j*" sound and thinking it's an "*h*."
- Pronouncing words with "*rr*" without rolling the "r's," such as saying "*caro*" (expensive) instead of "*carro*" (car).
- Pronouncing words with "*ll*" as if it were "*l*," such as saying "*polo*" (shirt) instead of "*pollo*" (chicken).
- Pronouncing words with "*ñ*" as if they were "*n*," such as saying "*cana*" (gray hair) instead of "*caña*" (cane).
- Mispronouncing words due to not understanding accentuation, such as saying "*esta*" (this) instead of "*está*" (is).
- Pronouncing the "*gue*" and "*gui*" in Spanish like "gway" and "gwee."
- Pronouncing the "*que*" and "*qui*" in Spanish like "kway" and "kwee."
- Forgetting that the "*z*" is pronounced as an "*s*" in Spanish.
- Forgetting that the "*v*" is pronounced more like a "*b*" in Spanish.

TEN MOST COMMON GRINGO GRAMMAR ERRORS

- Translating literally, such as saying "*Estoy frío.*" instead of "*Tengo frío.*" to express "I'm cold."
- Getting the gender of nouns mixed up, such as incorrectly saying "*la problema*" instead of "*el problema.*"
- Forgetting to reverse the order of adjectives and nouns in a sentence, such as saying "*grande casa*" instead of "*casa grande.*"
- Inserting "*por*" instead of "*para*" to always mean "for," such as saying "*Es por usted.*" instead of "*Es para usted.*" to express "It's for you."
- Distinguishing between the informal "*tú*" and the formal "*usted*" forms, such as addressing a stranger with "*¿Cómo estás tú?*" instead of "*¿Cómo está usted?*" (How are you?).
- Forgetting to apply a double negative, such as saying "*Hay nadie*" instead of "*No hay nadie*" to express "There is no one."
- Guessing incorrectly at cognate word translations, such as hearing "*sopa*" (soup) and thinking it means "soap."
- Overusing the subject pronouns, such as constantly adding "*yo*" (I) before verbs in a sentence even when it's already understood who's doing the talking.
- Mixing up the verbs, *ser* and *estar*, such as saying "*Estoy estudiante.*" instead of "*Soy estudiante.*" to express "I am a student."
- Applying regular verb conjugations upon irregular verbs, such as saying "*sabo*" instead of "*sé*" to express "I know."

Últimas palabras (Final Words)

It's entirely up to you how much *español* you'll eventually speak and understand. I hope that the easy-to-follow format has made your learning experience enjoyable—free of the stress and frustration of traditional programs. And probably by now you've discovered how the guidebook can be used to get best results. Use *Spanish for Gringos* any way you'd like! Set your own pace, take what you need, and reread only those pages that interest you. Some degree of language acquisition is guaranteed.

But this is really only the beginning. At the moment, you're merely crawling, standing, or staggering in the language. Trust me, fellow gringos, the best is yet to come.

Hasta luego, amigos,

Bill

GUIDE TO SPANISH SOUNDMAKING

A Quick-check Reference to Basic Pronunciation

- Spanish words are pronounced exactly the way they are written.
- Knowing the BIG 5 (vowels) is the key to speaking and understanding Spanish.
- Poor pronunciation in Spanish does not seriously effect communication, so do the best you can.
- Turn up the volume for the accented ( ) parts of words. Spanish words without accents get more volume at the end, *unless* they end in A, E, I, O, U, N, or S. These get more volume on the *next to the last part*.
- Spanish words are "run-together" in short, choppy pieces, usually pronounced in the front part of the mouth, with little or no air being used to make the sounds.

Translation Review!

Connect each word with its correct translation:

Colors	*Los colores*	**The class**	*La clase*
black	*morado*	book	*pluma*
green	*rojo*	pencil	*papel*
white	*verde*	paper	*libro*
purple	*negro*	table	*lápiz*
red	*blanco*	pen	*mesa*

Expressions	*Las expresiones*		
Good idea	*Quizás*	It's true	*Yo tampoco*
Me, too	*Creo que sí*	I'm so glad	*Con razón*
Maybe	*Sin duda*	No doubt	*Me alegro*
I think so	*Yo también*	Me, neither	*Es verdad*
No wonder	*Buena idea*	That's OK	*Está bien*

Questions	*Las preguntas*
What?	*¿Dónde?*
How much?	*¿Quién?*
Where?	*¿Qué?*
Who?	*¿Cuál?*
Which?	*¿Cuánto?*

Pronouns	*Los pronombres*
She	*Ellos*
He	*Ustedes*
We	*Él*
They	*Ella*
You guys	*Nosotros*

Numbers	*Los números*
10	*doce*
18	*treinta*
12	*diez*
15	*dieciocho*
30	*quince*

Days of the week	*Los días de la semana*
Monday	*miércoles*
Saturday	*domingo*
Sunday	*lunes*
Thursday	*sábado*
Wednesday	*jueves*

The weather	*El clima*
clear	*lluvia*
sun	*frío*
cold	*despejado*
snow	*nieve*
rain	*sol*

Feelings	*Los sentimientos*
well	*ocupado*
busy	*preocupado*
surprised	*bien*
angry	*sorprendido*
worried	*enojado*

Body parts	*Las partes del cuerpo*
back	*estómago*
throat	*espalda*
stomach	*dedo*
head	*pierna*
tooth	*cabeza*
leg	*rodilla*
eye	*cuello*
finger	*garganta*
neck	*ojo*
knee	*diente*

The family

La familia

father	hijo
sister	esposa
grandfather	tío
daughter	hermana
mother	marido
aunt	abuelo
uncle	hija
wife	tía
husband	madre
son	padre

Occupations

Las ocupaciones

chef	bombero
surgeon	cajero
student	campesino
gardener	cirujano
cashier	jardinero
teacher	estudiante
plumber	camarero
waiter	profesor
farmer	plomero
firefighter	cocinero

Work

El trabajo

contract	copiadora
mail	almacén
strike	fábrica
product	horario
tool	huelga
copier	correo
factory	herramienta
schedule	contrato
warehouse	producto

Descriptions	*Las descripciones*
bad	*equivocado*
old	*guapo*
good	*viejo*
tall	*malo*
handsome	*blando*
inexpensive	*rubio*
empty	*barato*
soft	*bueno*
wrong	*vacío*
blond	*alto*

The house	*La casa*
closet	*escoba*
dryer	*trapeador*
rug	*espejo*
curtains	*cortinas*
mop	*alfombra*
washer	*plancha*
broom	*lavadora*
mirror	*sábanas*
iron	*secadora*
sheets	*ropero*

Rooms	*Los cuartos*
bedroom	*sala*
basement	*cocina*
kitchen	*dormitorio*
living room	*baño*
bathroom	*sótano*

Tools	*Las herramientas*
screwdriver	*escalera*
hose	*rastrillo*
saw	*destornillador*
rake	*manguera*
ladder	*serrucho*

The city

La ciudad

library	*supermercado*
post office	*escuela*
shoe store	*biblioteca*
church	*gasolinera*
supermarket	*zapatería*
pharmacy	*tienda*
bakery	*correo*
store	*farmacia*
gas station	*panadería*
school	*iglesia*

Transportation

El transporte

train	*avión*
boat	*autobús*
bicycle	*tren*
bus	*bote*
airplane	*bicicleta*

Animals

Los animales

duck	*caballo*
bird	*gato*
dog	*pájaro*
horse	*perro*
cat	*pato*
sheep	*vaca*
mouse	*puerco*
cow	*oveja*
pig	*ratón*

Food

La comida

steak	*pollo*
cookie	*helado*
bread	*galleta*
ice cream	*bistec*
turkey	*pastel*
lobster	*pan*
pie	*pavo*
candy	*langosta*
butter	*dulce*
chicken	*mantequilla*

Drinks	*Las bebidas*
milk shake	*leche*
wine	*jugo*
coffee	*batido*
juice	*café*
milk	*vino*

Clothing	*La ropa*
shorts	*camisa*
jacket	*medias*
hat	*calzoncillos*
shirt	*pantalones*
stockings	*sombrero*
raincoat	*guantes*
belt	*falda*
gloves	*impermeable*
skirt	*cinturón*
pants	*chaqueta*

Shopping	*Las compras*
bill	*cupón*
discount	*venta*
sale	*cuenta*
price	*descuento*
coupon	*precio*

Commands	*Mandatos*
Speak!	*¡Cállese!*
Go!	*¡Coma!*
Shut up!	*¡Escriba!*
Write!	*¡Vaya!*
Come!	*¡Hable!*
Eat!	*¡Espere!*
Wake up!	*¡Siéntese!*
Sit down!	*¡Despiértese!*
Wait!	*¡Agárrelo!*
Grab it!	*¡Venga!*

Verbs	*Los verbos*
open	*llorar*
cry	*vender*
carry	*abrir*
sell	*viajar*
travel	*llevar*

More verbs	*Más verbos*
save	*gritar*
rest	*celebrar*
wish	*ahorrar*
bet	*traducir*
celebrate	*buscar*
break	*descansar*
enjoy	*disfrutar*
yell	*quebrar*
translate	*desear*
look for	*apostar*

When?	*¿Cuándo?*
yesterday	*ayer*
before	*ahorita*
tomorrow	*a veces*
right now	*antes*
sometimes	*mañana*

Where?	*¿Dónde?*
outside	*hacia*
far	*arriba*
up	*afuera*
down	*lejos*
towards	*abajo*

Sports	*Los deportes*
team	*estadio*
coach	*partido*
stadium	*equipo*
practice	*entrenador*
match	*práctica*

Toys	*Los juguetes*
blocks	*cometa*
skates	*rompecabezas*
ball	*cubos*
kite	*pelota*
puzzle	*patines*

Things	*Objetos*
pin	*desodorante*
lock	*cepillo*
box	*alfiler*
deodorant	*carta*
magazine	*caja*
letter	*cerradura*
tip	*revista*
comb	*propina*
brush	*peine*

APPENDIX

Vocabulary/*Vocabulario*

Most of the words introduced in *Spanish for Gringos* can be found in the appendix. Action word forms such as the "Command Words" and specialty vocabulary such as "Traditional Foods," are not part of the appendix. Such terms are listed by category in the Table of Contents.

El and *la* are given only when you might be uncertain which is required *(la acción, el ángel)*. Words that are the same or are both masculine and feminine are indicated by *el/la (el/la ayudante)*.

Note, too, that for convenience all verbs have been grouped under the "to" form on the English to Spanish side *(to allow, to answer, to arrange,* etc.).

You will also discover that some words may have multiple meanings or equivalents in the other language. However, the simple translations given here are general enough for basic conversational usage.

For more specific information, consult with a Spanish speaker, or refer to Barron's *Beginning Spanish Bilingual Dictionary*.

English–Spanish

a una, un
a little bit poco
a lot (*many*) muchos
a lot (*much*) mucho
a very little bit poquito
about acerca de
above encima
abuse abuso
account cuenta
action la acción
actress la actriz
address la dirección
afterwards después
again otra vez
against contra
agency agencia
agent agente
ahead adelante
AIDS el SIDA
air conditioning el aire acondicionado
airplane el avión
airport aeropuerto
all todo
almost casi
alone solo
along a lo largo de
already ya
also también
always siempre
American gringo, americano
and y
angel el ángel
angry enojado
animal el animal
anniversary aniversario
announcement anuncio
another otra, otro
ant hormiga
anxious ansioso
any cualquiera
anyone cualquiera persona
anywhere cualquiera parte
apartment apartamento
apple manzana
application la aplicación
appointment cita
April abril
apron el delantal

architect el/la arquitecto
area code código de área
around alrededor de
ashtray cenicero
asleep dormido
asphalt asfalto
assistant el asistente
astronaut el/la astronauta
at en
at last por fin
athlete el atleta
attic el desván
August agosto
aunt tía
auto insurance seguro de auto
auto racing automovilismo
available disponible
avenue avenida
awhile rato
baby el/la bebé
backward al revés
bag bolsa
bakery panadería
bald calvo
ball bola, pelota
balloon globo
banana plátano
bank banco
bar (*drinking*) cantina
barber shop peluquería
bargain ganga
baseball el béisbol
basement sótano
basic básico
basketball el básquetbol
bathrobe bata de baño
bathroom baño
bathtub tina
battery batería
bay bahía
bear (*animal*) oso
beautiful bello
because porque
bed cama
bedroom dormitorio
bee abeja
beer cerveza
before antes

behind detrás
bellboy el botones
belt el cinturón
besides además
between entre
Bible Biblia
bicycle bicicleta
big grande
biking ciclismo
bill cuenta
billion el billón
bird pájaro
birth nacimiento
birthday el cumpleaños
bitter amargo
black negro
blackboard el pizarrón
blame culpa
blanket cobija
bleach el blanqueador
blender licuadora
block (*city*) cuadra
blond rubio
blouse blusa
blue azul
boat barco
boating paseo en bote
boiled herrido
book libro
bookcase librero
boot bota
border frontera
bored aburrido
boss el jefe
both ambos
bottle botella
bottom fondo
bowling el boliche
box (*container*) caja
boxing boxeo
boyfriend novio
bracelet el brazalete
brakes frenos
branch rama
brave valiente
bread el pan
brick ladrillo
bride novia
bridge el puente

briefcase el maletín
briefly brevemente
bright brillante
bring traer
broken roto
brooch el broche
broom escoba
broth caldo
brother hermano
brother-in-law cuñado
brown pardo, café
brush cepillo
bucket el balde
buddy compañero
building edificio
bus el autobús
bus stop parada de autobús
bush arbusto
but pero
butter mantequilla
cabbage repollo
cab driver el taxista
cabinet el gabinete
cake torta
calendar calendario
camel camello
camera cámara
campgrounds campamento
can lata
can opener el abrelatas
candy el dulce
cap gorra
capital (*letter*) mayúscula
car carro
car lot el lote de carros
card (*playing*) carta
cardboard el cartón
carpenter carpintero
carrot zanahoria
cartoon caricatura
cashier cajero
cat gato
Catholic católico
cement cemento
cemetery cementerio
centimeters centímetros
Central America Centroamérica
certain cierto

chain cadena
chair silla
chalk tiza
championship campeonato
change cambio
chapter capítulo
check el cheque
checkers juego de damas
cheese queso
chef cocinero
cherry cereza
chess el ajedrez
chicken pollo
child niña, niño
chimney chimenea
China China
Christian cristiano
Christmas la Navidad
church iglesia
cigarette cigarrillo
circus circo
clarinet el clarinete
clean limpio
clever listo
client el cliente
climate clima, tiempo
climate change cambio
  climático
clock el reloj
closed cerrado
closet ropero
cloth tela
clothing ropa
cloud la nube
clown payaso
coach el entrenador
coast costa
cockroach cucaracha
coffee el café
coffeemaker cafetera
coin moneda
cold frío
comb el peine
command mandato
communism comunismo
community la comunidad
computer computadora
concert concierto
conditioner (air) el
  acondicionador
conference conferencia
congratulations felicitaciones
contract contrato
conversation la conversación
cook cocinar
cooked cocido
cookie galleta
copier copiadora
corn el maíz
corner esqina
correct correcto
correctly correctamente
couch sofá
countryside campo
couple pareja, par
coupon el cupón
court (sport) cancha
court la corte
cousin primo
cow vaca
coward el cobarde
crab cangrejo
crazy loco
cream crema
credit card tarjeta de crédito
crime el crimen
cross la cruz
Cuba Cuba
cup taza

curtain cortina
customs aduana
cute chulo
daily diario
dance el baile
dangerous peligroso
dark oscuro
dark-haired moreno
darling querido
date fecha
daughter hija
daughter-in-law nuera
dawn madrugada
day el día
day before yesterday
  anteayer
dead muerto
death la muerte
debit dèbito
deer venado
degrees grados
democracy democracia
dentist el dentista
deodorant el desodorante
description la descripción
desert desierto
desk escritorio
dessert el postre
detergent el detergente
detour la desviación
devil diablo
dialogue diálogo
diamond el diamante
dictionary diccionario
diet dieta
different diferente
difficult difícil
dining room el comedor
dirt tierra
dirty sucio
discount descuento
dish el traste
distance distancia
doctor el/la médico
dog perro
doll muñeca
dollar el dólar
domestic doméstico
door puerta
doorbell el timbre
dot punto
doubt duda
down payment el enganche
downtown centro
downward abajo
drawer el cajón
dress vestido
dresser el tocador
drink bebida
driver's license licencia de
  chofer
drug droga
drum el tambor
dry seco
dryer secadora
duck pato
dumb tonto
during mientras
dusk el anochecer
dust polvo
each cada
early temprano
earring el arete
east este
easy fácil
easy chair el sillón
effectively efectivamente
egg huevo
eight ocho

eighteen diez y ocho
eighty ochenta
election elección
electric eléctrico
electricity la electricidad
elegant elegante
elephant el elefante
elevator el elevador
eleven once
emergency emergencia
employee empleado
empty vacío
end el fín
enemy enemigo
engine el motor
engineer ingeniero
England Inglaterra
English inglés
enough bastante
entrance entrada
envelope el sobre
event evento
every day todos los días
everybody todos, todo el
  mundo
everywhere por todas partes
example ejemplo
excellent excelente
exercise ejercicio
exit salida
expensive caro
experience experiencia
factory fábrica
faith la fe
faithful fiel
fall (season) otoño
family familia
famous famoso
fan fanático
fantastic fantástico
far lejos
farm finca
farmer campesino
fat gordo
father el padre
father-in-law suegro
fault falta, culpa
favorite favorito
fear miedo
feather pluma
February febrero
fence cerca
few pocos
fiancé novio
field campo
fifteen quince
fifty cincuenta
fight pleito
finally finalmente, por fin
fireman bombero
fireworks fuegos artificiales
first primer, primero
fish pez, el
fish (cooked) pescado
fisherman el pescador
five cinco
five hundred quinientos
flag bandera
flavor el sabor
floor piso
floor tile baldosa
flower la flor
fly (insect) mosca
fog neblina
following siguiente
food comida
for para, por
for rent se alquila
for sale se vende

forest el bosque
fork el tenedor
form forma
forward adelante
four cuatro
fourteen catorce
forty cuarenta
France Francia
fresh fresco
Friday viernes
fried frito
friend amigo
friendly amistoso
from desde, de
frown ceño
frying pan la sartén
full lleno
fun la diversión
funny chistoso
furious furioso
furniture los muebles
furniture store mueblería
game juego
gang pandilla
garage el garaje
garden el jardín
gardener el jardinero
gardening jardinería
garlic ajo
gas station gasolinera
gate el portón
ghost el fantasma
giraffe jirafa
girlfriend novia
glass vidrio
glass (drinking) vaso
glove el guante
goat chivo
God Dios
gold oro
good bueno
good-bye adiós
government gobierno
grammar gramática
grams gramos
grandchild nieta, nieto
grandfather abuelo
grandmother abuela
grape uva
grapefruit toronja
grass pasto, hierba
gray gris
green verde
green bean judía verde
groom novio
guide el/la guía
guitar guitarra
gum el chicle
gymnasium gimnasio
haircut el corte de pelo
half la mitad, medio
hallway pasillo
ham el jamón
hamburger hamburguesa
hammer martillo
hand la mano
handkerchief pañuelo
handsome guapo
hanger gancho
hard (to touch) duro
hat sombrero
he él
health la salud
heart el corazón
heat el calor
heating la calefacción
heaven cielo
height estatura
helicopter helicóptero

hell   infierno
hello   hola
helper   el/la ayudante
her   ella, su
here   acá, aquí
hers   suyo, suya
highway   carretera
hill   cerro
him   él
hippopotamus   hipopótamo
his   su, suyo, suya
Hispanic   hispánico, hispano
holy   santo
homework   tarea
honest   honesto
honey   la miel
hope   esperanza
horse   caballo
horseback riding   montar a
   caballo
hose   manguera
hospital   el hospital
hot   caliente
hot (spicy)   picante
hot dog   perro caliente
house   casa
How many?   ¿Cuántos?
How much?   ¿Cuánto?
however   sin embargo
hug   abrazo
hundred   cien
hundreds   cientos
hunger   el hambre
hunting   caza
husband   esposo
I   yo
ice   hielo
ice cream   helado
if   si
immediately   inmediatamente
importance   importancia
important   importante
in   en
in front of   enfrente de
inches   pulgadas
incorrect   incorrecto
inexpensive   barato
information   la información
insect   insecto
inside   adentro
instrument   instrumento
intelligent   inteligente
interesting   interesante
interview   entrevista
introduction   la introducción,
   la presentación
iron   plancha
island   isla
jacket   chaqueta
jail   la cárcel
January   enero
Japan   el Japón
jar   frasco
jealous   celoso
Jesus Christ   Jesucristo
Jew   judío
jewel   joya
jewelry shop   joyería
job   trabajo
joke   el chiste
juice   jugo
July   julio
June   junio
jungle   selva
just   apenas
justice   justicia
key   la llave
kilogram (2.2 pounds)
   kilogramo

kilometer (5/8 of a mile)
   kilómetro
king   el rey
kiss   beso
kitchen   cocina
kite   el cometa
knapsack   mochila
knife   cuchillo
knot   nudo
ladder   escalera
lady   dama, señora
lake   lago
lamp   lámpara
language   el idioma, lengua
large   grande
last   último
last night   anoche
late   tarde
later   luego
Latin   latino
laughter   risa
laundromat   lavandería
law   la ley
lawyer   abogado
lazy   perezoso
leaf   hoja
left (direction)   izquierda
lemon   el limón
lemonade   limonada
length   longitud
less   menos
lesson   la lección
letter (alphabet)   letra
letter (mail)   carta
lettuce   lechuga
library   biblioteca
license plate   placa
lie (not true)   mentira
life   vida
light   la luz
light (not dark)   claro
likewise   igualmente
lion   el león
list   lista
liter   litro
living room   sala
lobster   langosta
lock   cerradura
long   largo
lost   perdido
love   el amor
lovely   hermoso
lover   el amante
low   bajo
lowercase (letter)   minúscula
luck   la suerte
magazine   revista
magic   magia
magnificent   magnífico
maid   criada
mail   correo
majority   mayoría
makeup   el maquillaje
mall   centro commercial
man   el hombre
manager   el gerente
manner   manera
map   mapa
marble (toy)   canica
March   marzo
marriage   matrimonio
marvelous   maravilloso
match   fósforo
maximum   máximo
May   mayo
meal   comida
mean   cruel
meaning   significado
meat   la carne

meat market   carnicería
mechanic   mecánico
medicine   medicina
medium   mediano
meeting   junta
member   miembro
message   recado
meter   metro
method   método
Mexico   México
microwave   el microondas
middle   medio
midnight   la medianoche
miles   millas
milk   la leche
milkshake   batido de leche
million   el millón
millionaire   millonario
mine   mío
minority   minoría
minute   minuto
miracle   milagro
mirror   espejo
Miss   señorita
mister   el señor
modern   moderno
moment   momento
Monday   lunes
money   dinero
monkey   mono
month   el mes
mop   el trapeador
more   más
mother   la madre
motorcycle   motocicleta
mouse   el ratón
movie   el cine
Mr.   sr. (abr. for señor)
Mrs.   sra. (abr. for señora)
mud   lodo
museum   museo
music   música
musician   músico
mustard   mostaza
my   mi, mis
nail   clavo
name   el nombre
napkin   servilleta
narrow   estrecho
nation   la nación
nationality   la nacionalidad
nature   naturaleza
near   cerca
necessary   necesario
necklace   el collar
needle   aguja
neighborhood   barrio
neither   tampoco
nervous   nervioso
net   la red
never   nunca
nevertheless   sin embargo
news   las noticias
newspaper   periódico
next   próximo, siguiente
nice   simpático
nightmare   pesadilla
nine   nueve
nine hundred   novecientos
nineteen   diez y nueve
ninety   noventa
no one   nadie
none   ninguna, ninguno
noon   el mediodía
North America   Norteamérica
notations   apuntes
note   nota
notebook   cuaderno
nothing   nada

notice   la notificación
November   noviembre
nowadays   ahora
nowhere   por ningún lado
number   número
nurse   enfermera
nut (food)   la nuez
obesity   la obesidad
obvious   obvio
ocean   océano
October   octubre
of   de
of the   del
offer   oferta
office   oficina
oil   el aceite
old   viejo
older   mayor
on   en
once   una vez
one   uno
onion   cebolla
only   sólo
open   abierto
operation   la operación
opposite   contrario
or   o
orange (fruit)   naranja
orange (color)   anaranjado
our   nuestra(s), nuestro(s)
out of order   descompuesto
outlet   el enchufe
outside   afuera
outskirts   las afueras
over   sobre
over there   allá
overcoat   abrigo
owner   dueño
page   página
pain   el dolor
paint   pintura
painter   el pintor
pair   par, pareja
pajamas   piyama
pants   los pantalones
paper   el papel
parents   los padres
park   el parque
parking   estacionamiento
party   fiesta
passionate   apasionado
passport   el pasaporte
past   pasado
payment   pago
pea   el guisante
peace   la paz
pearl   perla
pen   pluma
pencil   el lápiz
people   la gente
pepper   pimienta
perfectly   perfectamente
perfume   el perfume
person   persona
pharmacy   farmacia
philosophy   filosofía
phone number   númcro de
   teléfono
photo   la foto
photography   fotografía
pictures   los cuadros
pie   el pastel
pig   puerco
pillow   almohada
pin   el alfiler
pitcher   cántaro
place   el lugar, sitio
plant   planta
plastic   plástico

plate plato
playground patio de recreo
pleasant agradable
please por favor
pliers los alicates
plumber plomero
plumbing tubería
point punta
police policía
policy póliza
political party partido
politics política
pollution la contaminación
poor pobre
pork cerdo
possession la posesión
possible posible
post office (oficina de) correo
postcard tarjeta postal
pot olla
potato papa, patata
pounds libras
poverty pobreza
practice práctica
precious precioso
pregnant embarazada
presentation la presentación
president el presidente
pretty bonito
price precio
problem el problema
product producto
professional profesional
program programa
promise promesa
pronunciation la
  pronunciación
proud orgulloso
public público
punishment castigo
purple morado
purse bolsa
puzzle el rompecabezas
queen reina
question pregunta
quick rápido
quickly rápidamente
racket raqueta
rain lluvia
raincoat el impermeable
rake rastrillo
ranch rancho
rat rata
raw crudo
razor navaja
reading lectura
ready listo
reason la razón
receipt recibo
recipe receta
recreation recreo
red rojo
red-headed pelirrojo
refreshment refresco
refrigerator el refrigerador
relative el pariente
religion la religión
repair la reparación
reservation la reservación
respect respeto
restaurant el restaurante
restroom sanitario
review repaso
rhinoceros el rinoceronte
ribbon cinta
rice el arroz
rich rico
right (direction) derecha
right now ahora mismo

ring anillo
ripe maduro
river río
road camino
road sign la señal
robbery robo
rock roca
rocket el cohete
romantic romántico
room la habitación
rotten podrido
rough áspero
rubber goma
rug alfombra
sail navegar
saint santo
salad ensalada
salary sueldo
sale venta
salesperson el vendedor,
  vendedora
salt la sal
salty salado
salvaton la salvación
same mismo
same to you igualmente
sand arena
sangria sangría
Saturday sábado
sauce salsa
sausage salchicha
saw serrucho
saxophone saxófono, el
  saxofón
scarf bufanda
schedule horario
school escuela
scissors las tijeras
scooter trotineta
screw tornillo
screwdriver el destornillador
scuba diving buceo
sea el/la mar
season la estación
second segundo
secretary secretario
seed semilla
seesaw el sube y baja
sentence la frase
September septiembre
seven siete
seven hundred setecientos
seventeen diez y siete
seventy setenta
several varios
sex sexo
shampoo el champú
she ella
sheep oveja
sheet (bed) sábana
sheet (paper) hoja
shirt camisa
shoe zapato
shoe store zapatería
short (in height) bajo
short (in length) corto
shorts los calzoncillos
shovel pala
shower ducha
shrimp el camarón
shy tímido
sickness la enfermedad
side lado
sidewalk acera
signal light semáforo
silver plata
sincere sincero
sincerely sinceramente
single soltero

sister hermana
sister-in-law cuñada
site sitio, el lugar
six seis
sixteen diez y seis
sixty sesenta
size tamaño
skates los patines
ski esquiar
skill la habilidad
skirt falda
skyscraper el rascacielos
slippers las pantuflas
slow lento
slowly despacio
small chico
smile sonrisa
smoke humo
smooth suave
snake víbora
snow la nieve
so tan
soap el jabón
soccer el fútbol
social security seguro social
socks los calcetines
soft blando
soldier soldado
some algún, algunos, algunas;
  uno(s), una(s)
someone alguien
sometimes a veces
somewhere por algún lugar
son hijo
son-in-law yerno
soon pronto
soul el alma
sound sonido
soup sopa
sour agrio
South America Sudamérica
Spain España
Spanish español
special especial
spend gastar
spider araña
spoon cuchara
sport el deporte
sports coat saco
spring primavera
stadium estadio
stain mancha
stairs las escaleras
stamp sello
station la estación
steak el bistec
step paso
stereo estéreo
stick palo
still aún
stone piedra
store tienda
stove estufa
strange extraño
strawberry fresa
street la calle
strike huelga
strong fuerte
structure estructura
student el estudiante
studious aplicado
study estudio
stupid estúpido
subway metro, (abr. for
  metropolitano)
suddenly de repente
sugar el/la azúcar
suit el traje
suitcase maleta

summer verano
Sunday domingo
sunset puesta del sol
supermarket supermercado
sure seguro
surname apellido
surgeon cirujano
surprised sorprendido
sweater el suéter
sweatsuit el traje de
  entrenamiento
sweet dulce
sweethearts los novios
swimming pool piscina
swimsuit el traje de baño
symbol símbolo
T-shirt camiseta
table mesa
tablecloth el mantel
tall alto
taxes impuestos
tea el té
teacher maestro
team equipo
tear (crying) lágrima
telephone teléfono
television la televisión, el
  televisor
temperature temperatura
ten diez
tennis el tenis
terrible terrible
terrific terrífico
test el examen
thanks gracias
that que
that (there) esa, ese, eso
that (one) ésa, ése
the (f) la, las
the (m) el, los
their su, sus, suyos
theirs suyo
theme el tema
then entonces
there ahí
there is, there are hay
therefore por eso
these estos, estas
these ones éstos, éstas
they ellos, ellas
thief el ladrón
thin flaco
thing cosa
thirst la sed
thirteen trece
thirty treinta
this esto, esta, este
this one ésta, éste
those esos, esas
those (over there) aquéllos,
  aquéllas
thousand mil
thread hilo
three tres
throat garganta
Thursday jueves
ticket boleto
tide marea
tie corbata
tiger el tigre
time (hour) hora
time tiempo
tip propina
tire (auto) llanta
tired cansado
to a
to allow dejar
to answer contestar
to arrange arreglar

to arrive llegar
to attend asistir
to avoid evitar
to be ser
to be (location and condition)
  estar
to begin empezar
to bet apostar
to block obstruir
to break quebrar
to build construir
to camp acampar
to carry llevar
to cast lanzar, tirar
to catch coger
to celebrate celebrar
to chat platicar
to check revisar
to climb subir
to close cerrar
to collect coleccionar
to comb one's hair peinarse
to control controlar
to court someone pretender
to cry llorar
to cut cortar
to dance bailar
to develop desarrollar
to discuss discutir
to do hacer
to draw dibujar
to dream soñar
to drink beber, tomar
to enjoy oneself divertirse
to exit salir
to find encontrar
to finish terminar
to fish pescar
to fix reparar
to float flotar
to fly volar
to forget olvidar
to get dressed vestirse
to give dar
to guess adivinar
to happen suceder, pasar
to hate odiar
to have tener
to hit golpear, pegar
to import importar
to join juntar
to kiss besar
to learn aprender
to leave salir
to leave behind dejar
to lend prestar
to lie down acostarse
to listen escuchar
to look for buscar
to lose perder
to love amar
to make hacer

to make a call hacer una
  llamada
to miss faltar
to order ordenar
to park estacionar
to pass pasar
to pay pagar
to pitch lanzar
to plant plantar
to play (a game) jugar
to play (an instrument)
  tocar
to pull jalar
to push empujar
to put poner
to quit renunciar
to raise oneself up levantarse
to read leer
to receive recibir
to rest descansar
to return volver
to ride (on the back of an
  animal) montar
to run correr
to save (keep) ahorrar
to say decir
to sell vender
to show mostrar
to sing cantar
to sit down sentarse
to skate patinar
to sleep dormir
to smoke fumar
to speak hablar
to stick pegar, adherir
to survive sobrevivir
to swim nadar
to take tomar
to take advantage aprovechar
to take away quitar
to throw tirar
to touch tocar
to translate traducir
to travel viajar
to trust confiar
to try probar
to type escribir a máquina
to visit visitar
to walk caminar
to wash lavar
to watch mirar
to weigh pesar
to wish desear
to work trabajar
to yell gritar
to yield ceder
to the al
toaster tostador
today hoy
together juntos
toilet excusado
tomorrow mañana

tongue lengua, el idioma
too, also también
too much demasiado
tool herramienta
tourist el/la turista
towards hacia
towel toalla
town pueblo
traffic tráfico
train el tren
training entrenamiento
trash can el bote de basura
travel agency agencia de
  viajes
treasure tesoro
tree el árbol
truck el camión
truck driver camionero
truth la verdad
Tuesday martes
turkey pavo
twelve doce
twenty veinte
twin gemelo
two dos
typewriter máquina de
  escribir
umbrella el paraguas
underneath debajo
underwear ropa interior
United States Estados
  Unidos
university la universidad
until hasta
upward arriba
usually usualmente
vacation la vacación
vacuum cleaner la aspiradora
valley el valle
vase florero
very muy
very few poquitos
very pretty muy lindo
view vista
violence violencia
violent violento
violin el violín
vocabulary vocabulario
voice la voz
volleyball el vóleibol
vote voto
waiter mesero
waitress mesera
wallet cartera
war guerra
washbasin lavabo
washer la lavadora
watch el reloj
water el agua
wave ola
we nosotros, nosotras
weak débil

weapon el arma
weather tiempo, el clima
wedding boda
Wednesday miércoles
week semana
weight peso
welcome bienvenidos
well-mannered educado
What? ¿Qué?
When? ¿Cuándo?
Where? ¿Dónde?, ¿Adónde?
Which? ¿Cuál?
white blanco
Who? ¿Quién?
Why? ¿Por qué?
wide ancho
wife esposa
wild salvaje
window ventana
wine vino
wine and fruit juice sangría
winter invierno
wire el alambre
with con
with me conmigo
with you (between friends,
  family) contigo
with him/her/them consigo
without sin
woman la mujer
wood madera
word palabra
work trabajo
world mundo
writer el escritor
written escrito
wrong equivocado
yard patio
year año
yellow amarillo
yes sí
yesterday ayer
yet todavía, aún
you (between friends and
  family) tú
you usted
you guys ustedes
young joven
young man el joven
younger menor
your (between friends and
  family) tu
your su
yours suyo
yours (between friends and
  family) tuyo
zebra cebra
zero cero
zip code zona postal
zoo zoológico

Spanish–English

a to
a lo largo de along
a veces sometimes
abajo downward
abeja bee
abierto open
abogado lawyer
abrazo hug
abrelatas, el can opener
abrigo overcoat
abril April
abuela grandmother
abuelo grandfather
aburrido bored
abuso abuse
acá here
acamper to camp
acción, la action
aceite, el oil
acera sidewalk
acerca de about
acondicionador, el air conditioner
acostarse lie down
actríz, la actress
adelante ahead, forward
además besides
adentro inside
adherir to stick
adiós good-bye
adivinar guess
¿Adónde? Where?
aduana customs
aeropuerto airport
afuera outside
afueras, las outskirts
agencia agency
agencia de viajes travel agency
agente agent
agosto August
agradable pleasant
agrio sour
agua, el water
aguja needle
ahí there
ahora nowadays
ahora mismo right now

ahorrar save
aire acondicionado, el air conditioning
ajedrez, el chess
ajo garlic
al to the
al revés backward
alambre, el wire
alfiler, el pin
alfombra rug
alguien someone
algún, algunos, algunas some
alicates, los pliers
alma, el soul
almohada pillow
alrededor (de) around
alto tall
allá over there
amante, el lover
amar to love
amargo bitter
amarillo yellow
ambos both
americano American
amigo friend
amistoso friendly
amor, el love
anaranjado orange (color)
ancho wide
ángel, el angel
anillo ring
animal, el animal
aniversario anniversary
anoche last night
anochecer, el dusk
anteayer day before yesterday
antes before
anuncio announcement
año year
ansioso anxious
apartamento apartment
apasionado passionate
apellido surname
apenas just
aplicación, la application
aplicado studious
apostar to bet

aprender to learn
aprovechar to take advantage
apuntes, los notations
aquéllas, aquéllos those (over there)
aquí here
araña spider
árbol, el tree
arbusto bush
arena sand
arete, el earring
arma, el weapon
arquitecto architect
arreglar to arrange
arriba upward
arroz, el rice
asfalto asphalt
asistente, el assistant
asistir attend
áspero rough
aspiradora vacuum cleaner
astronauta, el astronaut
atleta, el athlete
aún still, yet
autobús, el bus
automovilismo auto racing
avenida avenue
avión, el airplane
ayer yesterday
ayudante, el helper
azul blue
azúcar, el sugar
bahía bay
bailar to dance
baile, el dance
bajo short (in height), low
balde, el bucket
baldosa floor tile
banco bank
bandera flag
baño bathroom
barato inexpensive
barco boat
barrio neighborhood
bastante enough
bata de baño bathrobe
batería battery
batido de leche milkshake

básico basic
básquetbol, el basketball
beber to drink
bebé, el baby
bebida drink
beisbol, el baseball
bello beautiful
besar to kiss
beso kiss
Biblia Bible
biblioteca library
bicicleta bicycle
bienvenidos welcome
billón, el billion
bistec, el steak
blanco white
blando soft
blanqueador, el bleach
blusa blouse
boda wedding
bola ball
boleto ticket
boliche, el bowling
bolsa bag, purse
bombero fireman
bonito pretty
bosque, el forest
bota boot
bote de basura, el trash can
botella bottle
botones, el bellboy
boxeo boxing
brazalete, el bracelet
brevemente briefly
brillante bright
broche, el brooch
buceo scuba diving
bueno good
bufanda scarf
buscar look for
caballo horse
cada each
cadena chain
café, el coffee
cafetera coffeemaker
caja box (container)
cajero cashier
cajón drawer

calcetines, los socks
caldo broth
calefacción, la heating
calendario calendar
caliente hot
calle, la street
calor, el heat
calvo bald
calzoncillos, los shorts
cama bed
cámara camera
camarón, el shrimp
cambio change
cambio climático climate change
camello camel
caminar to walk
camino road
camionero truck driver
camión, el truck
camisa shirt
camiseta T-shirt
campamento campgrounds
campesino farmer
campeonato championship
campo field, countryside
cancha court (sport)
cangrejo crab
canica marble (toy)
cansado tired
cantar to sing
cántaro pitcher
cantina bar (drinking)
capítulo chapter
la carcel jail
caricatura cartoon
carne, la meat
carnicería meat market
caro expensive
carpintero carpenter
carretera highway
carro car
carta playing card, letter (mail)
cartera wallet
cartón, el cardboard
casa house
casi almost
castigo punishment
católico Catholic
catorce fourteen
caza hunting
cebolla onion
cebra zebra
ceder to yield
celebrar to celebrate
celoso jealous
cementerio cemetery
cemento cement
cenicero ashtray
centímetros centimeters
centro downtown
Centroamérica Central America
Centro commercial mall
ceño frown
cepillo brush
cerca near; fence
cerdo pork
cereza cherry
cero zero
cerrado closed
cerradura lock
cerrar to close
cerro hill
cerveza beer
champú, el shampoo
chaqueta jacket
cheque, el check

chicle, el gum
chico small
chimenea chimney
China China
chiste, el joke
chistoso funny
chivo goat
chulo cute
ciclismo biking
cielo heaven
cien hundred
cientos hundreds
cierto certain
cigarrillo cigarette
cinco five
cincuenta fifty
cine, el movie
cinta ribbon
cinturón, el belt
circo circus
cirujano surgeon
cita appointment
clarinete, el clarinet
claro light (not dark)
clavo nail
cliente, el client
clima, el climate, weather
cobarde, el coward
cobija blanket
cocido cooked
cocina kitchen
cocinar to cook
cocinero chef
código del área area code
coger to catch
cohete, el rocket
coleccionar to collect
collar, el necklace
comedor, el dining room
cometa, la kite
comida food, meal
compañero buddy
computadora computer
comunidad, la community
comunismo communism
con with
concierto concert
conferencia conference
confiar to trust
conmigo with me
consigo with him/her/them
construir build
contaminación, la pollution
contestar to answer
contigo with you (between friends, family)
contra against
contrario opposite
contrato contract
controlar control
conversación, la conversation
copiadora copier
corazón, el heart
corbata tie
correctamente correctly
correcto correct
correo mail, post office
correr run
cortar to cut
corte de pelo, el haircut
corte, la court
cortina curtain
corto short (in length)
cosa thing
costa coast
crema cream
criada maid
crimen, el crime
cristiano Christian

crudo raw
cruel mean
cruz cross
cuaderno notebook
cuadra block (city)
cuadros, los pictures
¿Cuál? Which?
cualquiera any
cualquier parte anywhere
cualquier persona anyone
¿Cuándo? When?
¿Cuánto? How much?
¿Cuántos? How many?
cuarenta forty
cuatro four
Cuba Cuba
cucaracha cockroach
cuchara spoon
cuchillo knife
cuenta bill, account
culpa fault, blame
cumpleaños, el birthday
cuñada sister-in-law
cuñado brother-in-law
cupón, el coupon
dama lady
dar to give
de of, from
de repente suddenly
debajo underneath
débil weak
débito debit
decir to say
dejar to leave behind; to allow
del of the
delantal, el apron
demasiado too much
democracia democracy
dentista, el dentist
deporte, el sport
derecha right (direction)
desarrollar to develop
descansar to rest
descompuesto out of order, broken-down
descripción, la description
descuento discount
desde from
desear to wish
desierto desert
desodorante, el deodorant
despacio slowly
después afterwards
destornillador, el screwdriver
desván, el attic
desviación, la detour
detergente, el detergent
detrás behind
día, el day
diablo devil
diálogo dialogue
diamante, el diamond
diario daily
dibujar to draw
diccionario dictionary
dieta diet
diez ten
diez y nueve nineteen
diez y ocho eighteen
diez y seis sixteen
diez y siete seventeen
diferente different
difícil difficult
dinero money
Dios God
dirección, la address
discutir discuss
disponible available

distancia distance
diversión, la fun
divertirse to enjoy oneself
doce twelve
dólar, el dollar
dolor, el pain
doméstico domestic
domingo Sunday
¿Dónde? Where?
dormido asleep
dormir to sleep
dormitorio bedroom
dos two
droga drug
ducha shower
duda doubt
dueño owner
dulce sweet
dulce, el candy
duro hard (to touch)
edificio building
educado well-mannered
efectivamente effectively
ejemplo example
ejercicio exercise
él he, him
el the (m., sing.)
elección election
electricidad, la electricity
eléctrico electric
elefante, el elephant
elegante elegant
elevador, el elevator
ella she, her
ellos, ellas they
embarasada pregnant
emergencia emergency
empezar to begin
empleado employee
empujar to push
en at, in, on
encima above
encontrar to find
enchufe, el outlet
enemigo enemy
enero January
enfermedad, la sickness
enfermera nurse
enfrente de in front of
enganche, el down payment
enojado angry
ensalada salad
entonces then
entrada entrance
entre between
entrenador, el coach
entrenamiento training
entrevista interview
equipo team
equivocado wrong
esa, ese that
ésa, ése that one
esas, esos those
ésas, ésos those (there)
escalera ladder
escaleras, las stairs
escoba broom
escribir a máquina to type
escrito written
escritor, el writer
escritorio desk
escuchar to listen
escuela school
eso that
España Spain
español Spanish
especial special
espejo mirror
esperanza hope

esposa wife
esposo husband
esquiar ski
esquina, la corner
esta, este this
ésta, éste this one
estación, la season; station
estacionamiento, el parking
estacionar to park
estadio stadium
Estados Unidos United States
estar to be *(location and condition)*
estas, estos these
éstas, éstos these ones
estatura height
este east
esto this
estrecho narrow
estructura structure
estudiante, el student
estudio study
estufa stove
estúpido stupid
evento event
evitar to avoid
examen, el test
excelente excellent
excusado toilet
experiencia experience
extraño strange
fábrica factory
fácil easy
falda skirt
falta fault
faltar to miss
familia family
famoso famous
fanático fan
fantasma, el ghost
fantástico fantastic
farmacia pharmacy
favorito favorite
fe, la faith
febrero February
fecha date
felicitaciones congratulations
fiel faithful
fiesta party
filosofía philosophy
fin, el end
finalmente finally, at last
finca farm
flaco thin
flor, la flower
florero vase
flotar to float
fondo bottom
forma form
fósforo match
fotografía photograph, photography
Francia France
frasco jar
frase, la sentence
frenos brakes
fresa strawberry
fresco fresh
frío cold
frito fried
frontera border
fuegos artificiales fireworks
fuerte strong
fumar smoke
furioso furious
fútbol, el soccer
gabinete, el cabinet
galleta cookie

gancho hanger
ganga bargain
garaje, el garage
garganta throat
gasolinera gas station
gastar spend
gato cat
gemelo twin
gente, la people
gerente, el manager
gimnasio gymnasium
globo balloon
gobierno government
golpear to hit
goma rubber
gordo fat
gorra cap
gracias thanks
grados degrees
gramática grammar
gramos grams
grande big, large
gringo American
gris gray
gritar to yell
guante, el glove
guapo handsome
guerra war
guía, el/la guide
guisante, el pea
guitarra guitar
habilidad, la skill
habitación, la room
hablar to speak
hacer to do, to make
hacer una llamada to make a call
hacia towards
hambre, el hunger
hamburguesa hamburger
hasta until
hay there is, there are
helado ice cream
helicóptero helicopter
hermana sister
hermano brother
hermoso lovely
herramienta tool
herrido boiled
hielo ice
hija daughter
hijo son
hilo thread
hipopótamo hippopotamus
hispánico Hispanic
hispano Hispanic
hoja leaf, sheet *(paper)*
hola hello
hombre, el man
honesto honest
hora time *(hour)*
horario schedule
hormiga ant
hospital, el hospital
hoy today
huelga strike
huevo egg
humo smoke
idioma language; tongue
iglesia church
igualmente likewise, same to you
impermeable, el raincoat
importar to import
importancia importance
importante important
impuestos taxes
incorrecto incorrect
infierno hell

información, la information
ingeniero engineer
Inglaterra England
inglés English
inmediatamente immediately
insecto insect
instrumento instrument
inteligente intelligent
interesante interesting
introducción, la introduction
invierno winter
isla island
izquierda left *(direction)*
jabón, el soap
jalar to pull
jamón, el ham
Japón, el Japan
jardín, el garden
jardinería gardening
jardinero gardener
jefe, el boss
Jesucristo Jesus Christ
jirafa giraffe
joya jewel
joyería jewelery shop
joven young, young man
judía verde green bean
judío Jew
juego game
juego de damas checkers
jueves Thursday
jugar to play *(a game)*
jugo juice
julio July
junio June
junta meeting
juntar to join
juntos together
justicia justice
kilogramo kilogram *(2.2 pounds)*
kilómetro kilometer *(5/8 of a mile)*
la, las the *(f.)*
lado side
ladrillo brick
ladrón, el thief
lago lake
lágrima tear *(crying)*
lámpara lamp
langosta lobster
lanzar to pitch, to cast
lápiz pencil
largo long
lata can
latino Latin
lavabo washbasin
lavadora washer
lavandería laundromat
lavar to wash
lección, la lesson
lectura reading
leche, la milk
lechuga lettuce
leer to read
lejos far
lengua tongue, language
lento slow
león, el lion
letra letter *(alphabet)*
levantarse to raise oneself up
ley, la law
libras pounds
librero bookcase
libro book
licencia de chófer driver's license
licuadora blender
limón, el lemon

limonada lemonade
limpio clean
lista list
listo ready; clever
litro liter
loco crazy
lodo mud
longitud length
los the *(m., pl.)*
lote de carros, el car lot
luego later
lugar, el place, site
lunes Monday
luz, la light
llanta tire *(auto)*
llave, la key
llegar to arrive
lleno full
llevar to carry
llorar to cry
lluvia rain
madera wood
madre mother
madrugada dawn
maduro ripe
maestro teacher
magia magic
magnífico magnificent
maíz, el corn
maleta suitcase
maletín, el briefcase
mancha stain
mandato command
manera manner
manguera hose
mano, la hand
mantel, el tablecloth
mantequilla butter
manzana apple
mañana tomorrow
mapa, el map
maquillaje, el makeup
máquina de escribir typewriter
mar, el sea
maravilloso marvelous
marea tide
martes Tuesday
martillo hammer
marzo March
más more
matrimonio marriage
mayo May
mayor older
mayoría majority
mayúscula capital *(letter)*
máximo maximum
mecánico mechanic
mediano medium
medianoche midnight
medicina medicine
médico doctor
medio half, middle
mediodía, el noon
menor younger
menos less
mentira lie *(not true)*
mes, el month
mesa table
mesera waitress
mesero waiter
método method
metro *(abr. for* **metropolitano***)* meter, subway
México Mexico
mi, mis my
microondas, el microwave
miedo fear
miel, la honey

miembro member
mientras during
miércoles Wednesday
mil thousand
milagro miracle
millas miles
millonario millionaire
millón, el million
minoría minority
minúscula lowercase (letter)
minuto minute
mío, mía mine
mirar to watch
mismo same
mitad, la half
mochila knapsack
moderno modern
momento moment
moneda coin
mono monkey
montar to ride (on the back of
  an animal)
montar a caballo horseback
  riding
morado purple
moreno dark-haired
mosca fly (insect)
mostaza mustard
mostrar to show
motocicleta motorcycle
motor, el engine
mucho a lot (much)
muchos a lot (many)
mueblería furniture store
muebles, los furniture
muerte, la death
muerto dead
mujer, la woman
mundo world
muñeca doll
museo museum
música music
músico musician
muy very
muy lindo very pretty
nacimiento birth
nación, la nation
nacionalidad, la nationality
nada nothing
nadar to swim
nadie no one
naranja orange (fruit)
naturaleza nature
navaja razor
navegar sail
Navidad, la Christmas
neblina fog
necesario necessary
negro black
nervioso nervous
nieta, nieto grandchild
nieve, la snow
ninguna, ninguno none
niña, niño child
nombre, el name
Norteamérica North America
norteamericano American
  (U.S.)
nosotras, nosotros we
nota note
noticias, las news
notificación, la notice
novecientos nine hundred
noventa ninety
novia girlfriend, bride
noviembre November
novio boyfriend, fiancé,
  groom
novios, los sweethearts

nube, la cloud
nudo knot
nuera daughter-in-law
nuestra(s), nuestro(s) our
nueve nine
nuez, la nut (food)
número number
número de teléfono phone
  number
nunca never
o or
obesidad, la obesity
obstruir to block
obvio obvious
océano ocean
octubre October
ochenta eighty
ocho eight
odiar to hate
oferta offer
oficina office
ola wave
olvidar forget
olla pot
once eleven
operación, la operation
ordenar to order
orgulloso proud
oro gold
oscuro dark
oso bear (animal)
otoño fall (season)
otra, otro another
otra vez again
oveja sheep
padre, el father
padres, los parents
pagar to pay
página page
pago payment
pájaro bird
pala shovel
palabra word
palo stick
pan, el bread
panadería bakery
pandilla gang
pantalones, los pants
pantuflas, las slippers
pañuelo handkerchief
papa potato
papel, el paper
par pair, couple
para for
parada de autobús bus stop
paraguas, el umbrella
pardo brown
pareja couple, pair
pariente, el relative
parque, el park
partido political party
pasado past
pasaporte, el passport
pasar to pass, to happen
paseo en bote boating
pasillo hallway
paso step
pastel, el pie
pasto grass
patata potato
patinar to skate
patines, los skates
patio yard
patio de recreo playground
pato duck
pavo turkey
payaso clown
paz, la peace
pegar to hit, to stick

peinarse to comb one's hair
peine, el comb
peligroso dangerous
pelirrojo red-headed
pelota ball
peluquería barber shop
perder to lose
perdido lost
perezoso lazy
perfectamente perfectly
perfume, el perfume
periódico newspaper
perla pearl
pero but
perro dog
perro caliente hot dog
persona person
pesadilla nightmare
pesar to weigh
pescado fish (cooked)
pescador, el fisherman
pescar to fish
peso weight
pez, el fish
picante hot (spicy)
piedra stone
pimienta pepper
pintor, el painter
pintura paint
piscina swimming pool
piso floor
piyama pajamas
pizarrón blackboard
placa license plate
plancha iron
planta plant
plantar to plant
plástico plastic
plata silver
plátano banana
platicar to chat
plato plate
pleito fight
plomero plumber
pluma feather; pen
pobre poor
pobreza poverty
poco a little bit
pocos few
podrido rotten
policía police (force and
  person)
política politics
póliza policy
polvo dust
pollo chicken
poner to put
poquito a very little bit
poquitos very few
por for
por algún lugar somewhere
por eso therefore
por favor please
por fin at last, finally
por ningún lado nowhere
¿Por qué? Why?
por todas partes everywhere
porque because
portón, el gate
posesión, la possession
posible possible
postre, el dessert
práctica practice
precio price
precioso precious
pregunta question
presentación, la presentation;
  introduction
presidente, el president

prestar to lend
pretender to court someone
primavera spring
primer, primero, primera
  first
primo cousin
probar try
problema, el problem
producto product
profesional professional
programa, el program
promesa promise
pronto soon
pronunciación, la
  pronunciation
propina tip
próximo next
público public
pueblo town
puente, el bridge
puerco pig
puerta door
puesta del sol sunset
pulgadas inches
punta point
punto dot
que that
¿Qué? What?
quebrar to break
querido darling
queso cheese
¿Quién? Who?
quince fifteen
quinientos five hundred
quitar to take away
rama branch
rancho ranch
rápidamente quickly
rápido quick
raqueta racket
rascacielos, el skyscraper
rastrillo rake
rata rat
rato awhile
ratón, el mouse
razón, la reason
recado message
receta recipe
recibir to receive
recibo receipt
recreo recreation
red, la net
refresco refreshment
refrigerador, el refrigerator
reina queen
religión, la religion
reloj, el clock, watch
renunciar to quit
reparación, la repair
reparar to fix
repaso review
repollo cabbage
reservación, la reservation
respeto respect
restaurante, el restaurant
revisar to check
revista magazine
rey, el king
rico rich
rinoceronte, el rhinoceros
río river
risa laughter
robo robbery
roca rock
rojo red
romántico romantic
rompecabezas, el puzzle
ropa clothing
ropa interior underwear

ropero closet
roto broken
rubio blond
sábado Saturday
sábana sheet (*bed*)
sabor, el flavor
saco sports coat
sal, la salt
sala living room
salado salty
salchicha sausage
salida exit
salir to leave, to exit
salsa sauce
salud, la health
salvación, la salvation
salvaje wild
sangría sangria, wine and
   fruit juice
sanitario restroom
santo saint; holy
sartén, la frying pan
saxófono, el saxofón
   saxophone
se alquila for rent
se vende for sale
secadora dryer
seco dry
secretaria secretary
sed, la thirst
segundo second
seguro sure
seguro de auto auto
   insurance
seguro social social security
seis six
selva jungle
sello stamp
semáforo signal light
semana week
semilla seed
sentarse to sit down
señal, la road sign
señor, el mister, man
señora lady
señorita miss, young lady
septiembre September
ser to be
serrucho saw
servilleta napkin
sesenta sixty
setecientos seven hundred
setenta seventy
sexo sex
si if
sí yes
SIDA, el AIDS
siempre always
siete seven

significado meaning
siguiente following, next
silla chair
sillón, el easy chair
símbolo symbol
simpático nice
sin without
sin embargo however,
   nevertheless
sinceramente sincerely
sincero sincere
sitio site, place
sobre over, envelope
sobrevivir survive
sofá, el couch
soldado soldier
sola, solo alone
sólo only
soltero single
sombrero hat
sonido sound
sonrisa smile
soñar to dream
soñoliento sleepy
sopa soup
sorprendido surprised
sótano basement
Sr. (*abr. for* **señor**) Mr.
Sra. (*abr. for* **señora**) Mrs.
Srta. (*abr. for* **señorita**) Miss
su your; his; her; their
suave smooth
sube y baja, el seesaw
subir to climb
suceder to happen
sucio dirty
Sudamérica South America
suegro, el father-in-law
sueldo salary
sueño dream
suerte, la luck
suéter, el sweater
supermercado supermarket
suyo his, hers, yours, theirs
tamaño, el size
también too, also
tambor, el drum
tampoco neither
tan so
tarde late
tarea homework
tarjeta de crédito credit card
tarjeta postal postcard
taxista, el cab driver
taza cup
té, el tea
tela cloth
teléfono telephone
televisión, la television

televisor, el television
tema, el theme
temperatura temperature
temprano early
tenedor, el fork
tener to have
tenis, el tennis
terminar to finish
terrible terrible
terrífico terrific
tesoro treasure
tía aunt
tío uncle
tiempo time; weather
tienda store
tierra dirt
tigre, el tiger
tijeras, las scissors
timbre, el doorbell
tímido shy
tina bathtub
tirar to throw, to cast
tiza chalk
toalla towel
tocador, el dresser
tocar to touch; to play (*an
   instrument*)
todavía yet
todo all
todo el mundo everybody
todos everybody
todos los días every day
tomar take; drink
tonto dumb
tornillo screw
toronja grapefruit
torta cake
tostador, el toaster
trabajar to work
trabajo work, job
traducir to translate
traer to bring
tráfico traffic
traje, el suit
traje de baño, el swimsuit
traje de entrenamiento, el
   sweatsuit
trapeador, el mop
traste, el dish
trece thirteen
treinta thirty
tren, el train
tres three
trotineta scooter
tú you (*between friends and
   family*)
tu your (*between friends and
   family*)
tubería plumbing

turista, el/la tourist
tuyo yours
último last
una vez once
una, un a
unas, unos some
universidad, la university
uno one
usted you
ustedes you guys
usualmente usually
uva grape
vaca cow
vacación, la vacation
vacío empty
valiente brave
valle, el valley
varios several
vaso glass (*drinking*)
veinte twenty
venado deer
vendedor, el salesperson
vender to sell
venta sale
ventana window
verano summer
verdad, la truth
verde green
vestido dress
vestirse to get dressed
viajar to travel
víbora snake
vida life
vidrio glass
viejo old
viernes Friday
vino wine
violencia violence
violento violent
violín, el violin
visitar to visit
vista view
vocabulario vocabulary
volar to fly
vóleibol, el volleyball
volver to return
voto vote
voz, la voice
y and
ya already
yerno son-in-law
yo I
zanahoria carrot
zapatería shoe store
zapato shoe
zona postal zip code
zoológico zoo

English-Spanish Verb Lists

accept, to **aceptar**
add, to **agregar, añadir**
advance, to **avanzar**
advise, to **recomendar**
agree, to **convenir**
allow, to **permitir**
answer, to **contestar**
arrive, to **llegar**
ask for, to **pedir**
ask, to **preguntar**
assist, to **atender**
attend, to **asistir**
be able to, to **poder**
be born, to **nacer**

be, to **estar, ser**
beg, to **suplicar**
begin, to **comenzar, empezar**
believe, to **creer**
belong, to **pertenecer**
bend, to **doblar**
bite, to **morder**
boil, to **hervir**
break, to **quebrar, romper**
breathe, to **respirar**
bring, to **traer**
build, to **construir**
buy, to **comprar**
call, to **llamar**

carry, to **llevar**
catch, to **atrapar**
change, to **cambiar**
charge, to **cargar**
choose, to **escoger**
clean, to **limpiar**
climb, to **subir**
close, to **cerrar**
collect, to **coleccionar**
come, to **venir**
confuse, to **confundir**
consider, to **considerar**
contain, to **contener**
convince, to **convencer**

cook, to **cocinar**
correct, to **corregir**
cost, to **costar**
count, to **contar**
cover, to **cubrir, tapar**
crash, to **chocar**
cross, to **cruzar, atravesar**
cry, to **llorar**
cut, to **cortar**
dance, to **bailar**
decide, to **decidir**
deliver, to **entregar**
deny, to **negar**
describe, to **describir**

desire, to **desear**
destroy, to **destruir**
die, to **morir**
dig, to **excavar**
discover, to **descubrir**
discuss, to **discutir**
divide, to **dividir**
do, to **hacer**
draw, to **dibujar**
dream, to **soñar**
drink, to **beber, tomar**
drive, to **manejar**
dry, to **secar**
earn, to **ganar**
eat, to **comer**
empty, to **vaciar**
end, to **acabar, terminar**
enter, to **entrar**
event **evento**
examine, to **examinar**
explain, to **explicar**
fall, to **caer**
fear, to **temer**
feed, to **alimentar**
feel, to **sentir**
fight, to **pelear**
fill, to **llenar**
find, to **encontrar**
find out, to **averiguar**
fish, to **pescar**
fit, to **caber**
fix, to **componer**
fly, to **volar**
follow, to **seguir**
forget, to **olvidar**
forgive, to **perdonar**
freeze, to **congelar**
get down, to **bajar**
get near, to **acercar**
get, to **obtener**
give, to **dar**
go, to **ir**
go out, to **salir**
greet, to **saludar**
grind, to **moler**
grow, to **crecer**
hang, to **colgar**
happen, to **suceder**
hate, to **odiar**
have, to **tener**
hear, to **oír**
help, to **ayudar**
hide, to **esconder**

hire, to **contratar**
hit, to **pegar**
hold, to **sostener**
hug, to **abrazar**
hunt, to **cazar**
hurt, to **doler**
imagine, to **imaginar**
include, to **incluir**
injure, to **herir**
insert, to **meter**
insist, to **insistir**
install, to **instalar**
interpret, to **interpretar**
invest, to **invertir**
judge, to **juzgar**
jump, to **saltar**
keep, to **guardar**
kick, to **patear**
kiss, to **besar**
know (someone), to **conocer**
know (something), to **saber**
lay, to **colocar**
lead, to **guiar**
learn, to **aprender**
leave, to **salir**
lend, to **prestar**
let, to **permitir**
lie, to **mentir**
lift, to **levantar**
light, to **encender**
like, to **gustar**
listen, to **escuchar**
live, to **vivir**
look, to **mirar**
loosen, to **soltar**
lose, to **perder**
love, to **amar**
maintain, to **mantener**
make, to **hacer**
mark, to **marcar**
mean, to **significar**
measure, to **medir**
meet, to **encontrar**
move, to **mover**
need, to **necesitar**
notify, to **notificar**
obey, to **obedecer**
obtain, to **obtener**
offer, to **ofrecer**
open, to **abrir**
oppose, to **oponer**
order, to **ordenar**
owe, to **deber**

park, to **estacionar**
pay, to **pagar**
permit, to **permitir**
persist, to **persistir**
pick up, to **recoger**
plant, to **plantar**
play, to **jugar**
plug in, to **enchufar**
polish, to **bruñir, pulir**
practice, to **practicar**
pray, to **rezar**
prefer, to **preferir**
prepare, to **preparar**
prevent, to **prevenir**
promise, to **prometer**
pronounce, to **pronunciar**
protect, to **proteger**
prove, to **probar**
pull, to **jalar**
push, to **empujar**
put, to **poner**
quit, to **renunciar**
rain, to **llover**
reach, to **alcanzar**
read, to **leer**
receive, to **recibir**
recognize, to **reconocer**
recommend, to **recomendar**
reduce, to **reducir**
refer, to **referir**
remember, to **recordar**
rent, to **alquilar**
repair, to **reparar**
repeat, to **repetir**
require, to **requirir**
rest, to **descansar**
retire, to **retirar**
return, to **devolver**
ride, to **montar**
run, to **correr**
sail, to **navegar**
save, to **ahorrar**
say, to **decir**
scratch, to **rascar**
search, to **buscar**
see, to **ver**
seem, to **parecer**
select, to **seleccionar**
sell, to **vender**
send, to **enviar, mandar**
serve, to **servir**
set, to **colocar**
sew, to **cocer**

shake, to **sacudir**
share, to **compartir**
shoot, to **disparar**
shout, to **gritar**
show, to **mostrar**
sing, to **cantar**
skate, to **patinar**
sleep, to **dormir**
smoke, to **fumar**
snow, to **nevar**
speak, to **hablar**
spend, to **gastar**
stay, to **quedar**
stir, to **batir, revolver**
study, to **estudiar**
subtract, to **restar**
sweep, to **barrer**
swim, to **nadar**
take care of, to **cuidar**
take out, to **sacar**
take, to **tomar**
talk, to **hablar**
teach, to **enseñar**
tell, to **decir**
thank, to **agradecer**
think, to **pensar**
threaten, to **amenazar**
throw, to **tirar**
touch, to **tocar**
translate, to **traducir**
travel, to **viajar**
try, to **tratar**
turn around, to **voltear**
turn off, to **apagar**
turn on, to **prender, encender**
understand, to **comprender, entender**
use, to **usar**
visit, to **visitar**
vote, to **votar**
walk, to **caminar, andar**
want, to **querer**
wash, to **lavar**
wear, to **llevar**
win, to **ganar**
wish, to **desear**
work, to **trabajar**
worry, to **preocupar**
write, to **escribir**

The Reflexives

bathe, to **bañarse**
become, to **hacerse**
brush, to **cepillarse**
change address, to **mudarse**
comb, to **peinarse**
complain, to **quejarse**
dress, to **vestirse**
fall asleep, to **dormirse**
fall down, to **caerse**

forget about, to **olvidarse**
get angry, to **enojarse**
get better, to **mejorarse**
get sick, to **enfermarse**
get married, to **casarse**
get ready, to **arreglarse**
get up, to **levantarse**
have a good time, to **divertirse**

hurry up, to **darse prisa**
leave, to **irse**
lie down, to **acostarse**
make a mistake, to **equivocarse**
make fun of, to **burlarse**
put on, to **ponerse**
realize, to **darse cuenta de**
remember, to **acordarse**

remove, to **quitarse**
shave, to **afeitarse**
sit down, to **sentarse**
stand up, to **pararse**
stay, to **quedarse**
wake up, to **despertarse**
wash, to **lavarse**
worry about, to **preocuparse**

Personal Success Chart

Date　　　　*Mi experiencia*

_____

　　　　　　I used a greeting!

_____

　　　　　　I understood my Spanish-speaking neighbor!

_____

_____

_____

_____

_____

_____

Notes

Tracks

31901056823398